# MILITARY
## PHOTOGRAPHS

### & How to
### Date Them

# MILITARY
## PHOTOGRAPHS

## *& How to Date Them*

## Neil Storey

COUNTRYSIDE BOOKS
NEWBURY BERKSHIRE

First published 2009
© Neil Storey 2009

COUNTRYSIDE BOOKS
3 Catherine Road
Newbury, Berkshire

To view our complete range of books,
please visit us at
www.countrysidebooks.co.uk

ISBN 978 1 84674 152 4

Designed by Peter Davies, Nautilus Design
Produced through MRM Associates Ltd., Reading
Printed by Information Press, Oxford

All material for the manufacture of this book
was sourced from sustainable forests

# Contents

# Introduction

By the sheer numbers involved serving in the First and Second World Wars, and the long history of Britain's armed forces, it would be almost impossible for any extended family tree not to have had some relative at some time in the army, the navy or the air force.

In the absence of a definite identity, or arm of service, of that serviceman or woman in your family album, or if you need to narrow down the options should you have, for example, ancestor brothers who all looked alike, or wonder if that photograph actually *is* Grandad, then I hope this book will be able to help you. For those of you with photos that you know are of your relatives but have wondered what the badges and insignia they are wearing signify, then again I hope this volume will interpret them for you. It could provide a more accurate date for when the photograph was taken, or help you to look for the clues to whether, for example, he was a Regular, Territorial or Service Battalion soldier, and aid further research with the select bibliography and websites listed at the back of this book. Just remember, it is a guide for people who want the basics and, I hope, a little more. It is designed to help you to understand and interpret your family military photographs and take your research further – it does not pretend to be encyclopaedic.

A good working knowledge of military uniforms, headdresses, badges, insignia and equipment cannot be acquired overnight. Indeed, I am still making revealing discoveries after working for over 25 years in the field and I know many who have been studying it far longer who are still learning too. The problem is that there will often be a particular regiment, battalion, company, platoon or even single man who proves a generalisation wrong! And be careful – one's memory can play tricks too – just because Grandad said it was so, it may or *may not* be the case, so always check oral history and especially family stories against official records if you can, before embarking on research.

If you know the name of your ancestor, so much research can be done online now. If they were a wartime casualty, they can be looked up on the Commonwealth War Graves Commission Debt of Honour Register; a record that often not only lists the name, rank, regiment and date of death but also where they are buried and often the actions fought around that particular cemetery. Medal index cards are kept by The National Archives; if you have the name of your ancestor, if he or she served overseas during the First World War they would have been entitled to service medals and (hopefully) their medal index card can be found online and, for a small fee, a copy of the card supplied direct to your computer (this service, including views of the backs of the card which may contain next of kin details, is also available from other fee-paid online family history research sites). The medal index card will state the regiments or corps in which he or she served, the medals to which they were entitled, and will show whether they were given an Honourable Discharge after sickness or wounding and thus entitled to a Silver War Badge (SWB).

If so entitled, the record deposited by the Ministry of Pensions, now also online at The National Archives, may provide a revealing amount of information about your ancestor. In the course of my research, I have encountered such records having as many as ten to twenty sheets of medical reports, service records and attestation papers. If your ancestor was a Commissioned Officer his papers may also survive and these are well worth acquiring

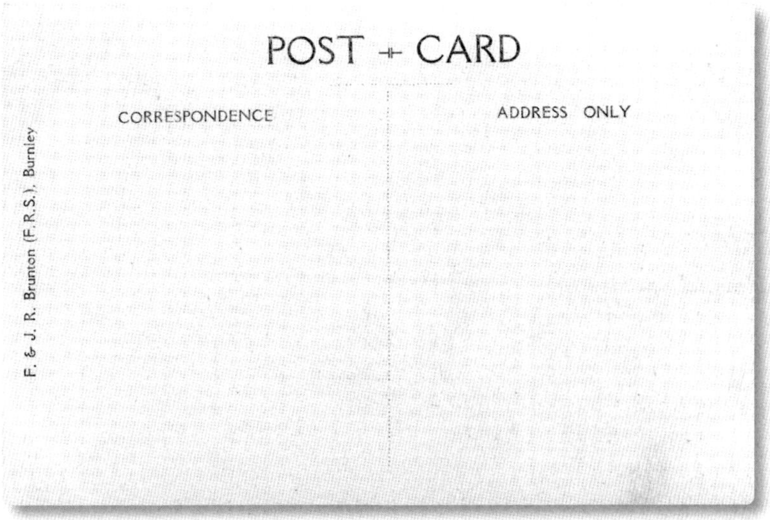

POST + CARD

CORRESPONDENCE     ADDRESS  ONLY

F. & J. R. Brunton (F.R.S.), Burnley

Always look beyond the portrait on your military postcards. If it is embossed or printed with the photographer's details and you can discern the unit from the cap badge, refer to Brigadier E.A. James' *British Regiments 1914-18* and you will stand a good chance of finding the battalion of the regiment he was serving with at the time.

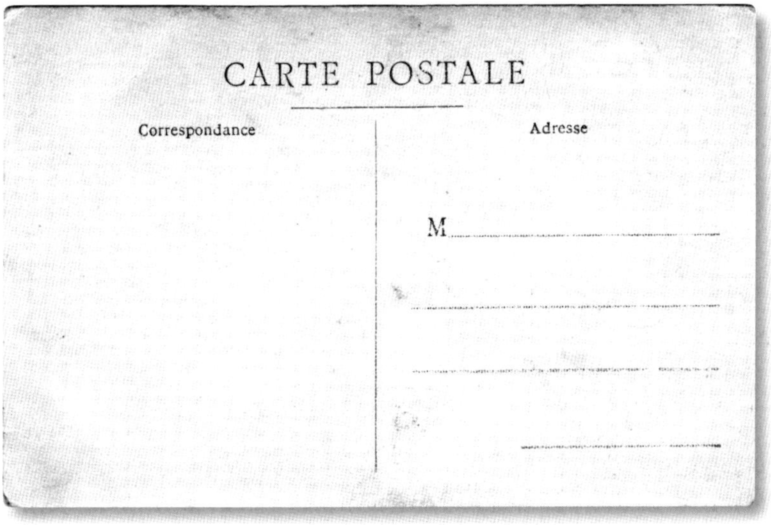

CARTE  POSTALE

Correspondance     Adresse

M

A typical Carte Postale postcard reverse on a portrait photograph of a British soldier taken in France during the First World War.

from The National Archives. Again, these will have attestation papers, correspondence, information about whether your ancestor was wounded, post-war correspondence and, if taken prisoner of war, he may well have had to give a written statement of the circumstances of his capture. But a word of caution: if your ancestor also served in the Second World War, his First World War papers will be lodged with those from the later conflict and, at the time of writing, the papers from that war have not yet been released.

Armed with such information as service records and medal index cards you have a good start in tracing your family military history, and this will also enhance the interpretation of any family military photographs.

The Royal Navy, the 'Senior Service', has its own unique traditions in uniforms and dress codes. From the mid-19th century to the middle of the 20th century when one observes family naval uniform photographs, in essence, very little changed for officers or men. What changes there were, were subtle. The size of the crowns atop naval caps reduced in size from the 19th to the 20th century, whereas the peaked caps worn by senior ratings and officers, rather like those of the military, moved from small peaks and very little crown to wider peaks and crowns. The wide-brimmed straw hats worn by sailors in hot climes were discontinued by the 1920s. The type of photograph, be it carte-de-visite, cabinet card or postcard (postcards were only produced from the early 20th century) can also be of great assistance in dating these and indeed all military photographs. However, the best clues to the history of your Royal Navy ancestor are to be found upon his uniform with his qualification badges (all of which would have been noted on his parchment service record with the date the qualification was achieved) and, of course, his cap tally which, at least in peacetime, names the ship upon which he was serving. From research into that one ship a fascinating history can often be discovered.

I realise not everyone is keen on computers, but library staff are very helpful if you want to search via a computer at your local library and there is a list of useful websites at the end of the book. I have also included a select bibliography of books I have used myself (especially in the days before the internet) and have readily obtained them from county library services for my students.

Above all, take your time. Examine your pictures carefully, enlarge them on the computer or use a magnifying glass. Even the identity of a blurred or indistinct badge may be confirmed by diligent research in relevant, well-illustrated books about cap badges such as those by Cox or Gaylor. Don't be afraid to write to the relevant armed force, regimental or corps museum of your ancestor to see if they can help, particularly if you know the battalion or a ship on which he or she served. Most local libraries will have access to a book listing museums from across the country; such information can also be looked up online. Many military museums now have online resources and advice for family historians researching ancestors in that particular regiment. But again, please be prepared to find that their responses can be variable – some excellent and well informed while others, sadly, less so.

Also look at clues beyond the portrait photograph, such as the address of the photographic studio often printed or embossed on the original photograph. Even if no photographer's name is shown, if the back of the card is marked 'Carte Postale' it indicates it was taken abroad; there may even be a censor mark and a message to help you. In the Second World

War, portrait photographs were often date-stamped at the studio.

Another often revealing avenue for research can be Rolls of Honour. It is not widely known that many villages, towns and cities compiled their own Rolls of Honour, not just of those who fell but also those who served. Village and small town rolls are often displayed in their local churches or are held in church records. Many large town and city Rolls of Honour are held in their central libraries. In some areas the local press published weekly images of 'Our boys at the front' and 'Serving King and County' features with small photographs of the local lads and lasses 'doing their bit'. Letters home were often sent in by families for publication, so the precious and now lost letters of your ancestor may just be waiting for you to discover them again in print on the pages of the old newspapers held at the local studies library near where they lived. Schools also maintained Rolls of Honour for the fallen and all who served; these can be found particularly at public and grammar schools but many state schools also produced their own, some even erected war memorials to fallen old boys.

Even if we personally remember some of our military ancestors, many of them would not talk of their experiences while on active service. Perhaps a few anecdotes of the good times would be forthcoming, but no more and so it was until the day they rejoined the comrades they left so long ago. The uniformed photographs that are now in our care, of them and the ancestors we never knew, bear mute testimony to often young men and women embarking on a great adventure, especially in the early war years. Some show groups of smiling comrades, several of whom probably did not return. Others taken during or at the end of the war show men changed by their experiences, somehow more serious, harder, their youth lost and aware of many comrades fallen. With sensible and diligent research I hope your images will be 'unlocked' and some of the stories of those often all too silent heroes will be revealed by the military photographs we all cherish so dearly.

*Neil R. Storey*

# Acknowledgements

Geoff Caulton; Robert Skinner; Richard Knight; Robert Bell; Margaret Newman, Royal Naval Museum Library, Portsmouth; Ian Hook, The Essex Regiment Museum; Michael Cornwell, The Rifles (Berkshire and Wiltshire) Museum; The Fusilier's Museum of Northumberland; Norfolk Family History Society; Helen Tovey, *Family Tree Magazine*.

Picture Credits: Geoff Caulton (page 15, No.2); Richard Knight (page 79, No.27 and page 87, No.37); Lilian Ream Collection (page 160 (No.16) and page 182 (No. 48)

All other images in this book are from originals in the author's collection.

RSM H.W. Pamplin, one of the King's Body Guard of the Yeoman of the Guard, the oldest British Military Corps still in existence, photographed in 1909.

# The Soldiers & Sailors of the Queen

## 1865-1900

Her Majesty Queen Victoria reigned for a total of 63 years and 7 months, an unparalleled rule of any British monarch before or since. She was the ruler of the British Empire, the greatest the world had ever witnessed. Truly it could be said it was an Empire upon which the sun never set and the greatest spectacle of her Empire was her military forces, both British Army and Colonial.

This book begins in the 1860s and 1870s – when the earliest family photographs start to appear – when regiments of the British Army were still designated by numbers, such as the 3rd Regiment of Foot, 9th Regiment of Foot etc. Head-dress badges usually displayed a regimental number (photographs 2, 3), and a complete list of the 99 British Line Infantry regiments (numbers above 100 existed but relate to colonial and training regiments) is given in Appendix I.

The British Victorian soldier was supremely distinctive; in the 1860s and 1870s scarlet tunics were still worn for both parades and field operations. Khaki was known to be worn by some regiments from as early as the Indian Mutiny in 1858, but was only formally introduced for wear by British units in India in 1878 (1).

The Glengarry, initially introduced as the Undress cap for Scottish regiments in 1852, was adopted by the majority of English line infantry regiments in plain blue in the 1870s and remained the standard headgear for other ranks (OR) soldiers up to the 1890s (1, 9). The iconic 'blue cloth' Home Service helmets (10, 12) were introduced in 1878, bidding farewell to the last of the shako pattern headgear. The 'quilted' shako head-dress can be dated to the years 1861-69 (3, 4). The shako was of blue cloth; the peak, binding and chin strap was patent leather. It was quilted inside (thus the nickname) to hold the stiffening of the shako in place. Several versions of the forage or Undress cap, introduced in the 1850s, can also be seen in early photographs (2, 6, 8).

By the 1860s fixed epaulettes for officers below field rank (2) had been superseded and insignia denoting rank, such as pips or crowns, were displayed on the collar. Gorgets and cross belts had been superseded by waist belts and sword hangers, and the sash worn around the waist by generations of British officers back to the 18th century was now worn from the left shoulder (2), held in place with a crimson cord of twisted silk, to the right hip (the same also applied to senior NCOs but worn right to left).

Most British Rifle Volunteer battalions adopted shakos and uniforms made from a distinctive grey material (4). These uniforms have occasionally misled a modern family historian to think the photograph of their ancestor showed them in the uniform of a Confederate soldier serving in the American Civil War. The lace on the cuffs was usually red or green, their pom-poms red, red and white, or green. Rifle Volunteers were also issued with Inverness-pattern cloaks or large plain grey coats made with a hood copied from French military designs.

The greatest changes in the British Army during the 19th century were introduced by the Secretary of State for War (and former soldier) Edward Cardwell between 1868 and 1874. Under Cardwell's localisation scheme, the country was divided into 66 Brigade Districts (later renamed Regimental Districts), based on county boundaries and population density. All line infantry regiments would now consist of two battalions sharing a Depot and associated recruiting area. One battalion would serve overseas, while the other was stationed at home for training. The Militia of the area usually became the third battalion.

Cardwell's reforms were continued by Secretary of State for War, Hugh Childers. In 1881 regimental seniority numbers were officially abolished and battalions came to be known by their number within the regiment and the regimental district name, and a number of corps of rifle volunteers were to be designated as volunteer battalions. It must be noted that, as ever, with the British Army, change was not always embraced wholeheartedly and many regiments were still referred to by their numbers, by their officers and men proud of their tradition. Regiments with long-established nicknames, such as 'The Buffs' and 'The Black Watch', lobbied to keep their distinctive names as part of their battalion titles.

During the late 1870s regimental numbers rather than devices can be found on blue cloth helmets and from 1881 the regimental device can be observed in the helmet plate centre. Regular Army officers' helmets (12) had a gilt binding along the front peak of the helmet and gilt fittings. The Victorian crown and star badge backing remained universal, but the gilt laurels would have a silvered scroll bearing the name of the regiment, e.g. The King's Own Yorkshire Light Infantry, and a regimental badge in the centre surrounded by a Royal Garter bearing the motto: 'Honi Soit Qui Mal-y-Pense'.

Other ranks (9, 10) wore a two-part helmet plate of a star surmounted with a Victorian crown, with a helmet plate centre with the name of the regiment in the circle and regimental device in the middle. Their helmets were bound around the brim with patent leather, with fixtures, fittings and helmet plate in brass or white metal for Volunteers. Some Volunteer battalions had a crown and helmet plate cast as one badge.

Line infantry, Rifle regiments and their Volunteer battalions all wore spikes on the top of their helmets (12) – Corps were denoted by balls. The helmet was made of cork and covered with blue cloth for line infantry or in rifle green for Rifle regiments and rifle Volunteers.

In 1880 officers' rank distinctions were removed from the collar and displayed on twisted gold shoulder cords instead (12). Colonels now had a crown and two stars, lieutenant colonels a crown and one star, a major a crown, a captain two stars, a lieutenant one, and a second lieutenant no stars. In their place on the collar was a further depiction of a regimental device on a collar badge.

Gone by the mid 1880s was the variety of regimental uniform distinctions and affectations; standardisation was the new regime (9, 10). Regimental facing colours were out for most; collar and cuffs were changed to white for English regiments, yellow for Scottish, green for Irish and blue for Royal regiments (though The Buffs and Suffolk Regiments had resumed their traditional facings by 1894). Other ranks' buttons all bore the heraldic lion and unicorn supporters, Royal Arms and Victorian crown. Belt buckles were standardised to the generic crown and lion in a circlet bearing the legend 'Dieu et Mon Droit'.

Uniforms for other ranks were the standard seven-button scarlet tunic with standing collar with rounded fronts, and 'jam pot' cuffs, edged with white down the left front (10). Chevron pointed cuffs on a tunic (3), rather than the jam-pot cuffs introduced in 1881, are an indicator of earlier period uniforms. There was also a lighter weight serge frock jacket with just five buttons, no white piping and no 'jam pot' cuffs, often issued for foreign service and then worn at home by returned troops. Up to the early 20th century British Army units wore valise pattern equipment that was pipe-clayed white (unless worn by Rifle regiments who polished theirs black).

To distinguish the Volunteer battalions from regulars, all buttons, badges and fittings were in white metal, and private soldiers and junior NCOs had white cord Austrian knots over their cuffs. Senior NCOs had white small chevron cuffs trimmed with black lace and Austrian knots (11).

Many soldiers at this time are photographed carrying swagger canes (9). These do not denote rank or special duties; all soldiers were expected to be proficient in 'stick drill' and to carry a cane when 'walking out'.

Mounted officers were permitted to wear riding breeches and knee boots (14). Regulations stipulated officers' boots were to be 'black or brown leather; mounted officers may wear knee boots or butcher boots with spur rests...provided that all officers of a unit be dressed alike.'

And so apparelled and equipped, the British Army dressed smartly for parades and duties and finally adopted khaki for operational service, fighting Queen Victoria's campaigns and garrisoning the Empire.

As mentioned in the Introduction, the uniform of the Royal Navy changed hardly at all over the 19th century. The cap tally – as per 1890 RN Dress Regulations 'worn with the name straight in front and tied with a bow over the ear' – will be the greatest help for family historians (15, 16). The lanyards worn (15) were originally used to fire the cannons on board ship, but by the later 19th century the sailors would carry their knives with them. Regulations on dress were precise (17): 'All frocks and jumpers are to be cut down ten inches from the collar, the strings being eight inches long; and on no account is any deviation from this to be permitted.'

Then, right at the end of Victoria's reign a war broke out in South Africa that would not only lead to numerous new developments and improvements in uniforms and equipment, but caused the British Army, and the Navy, to take a good look at itself, its men and how they were trained.

*1*

**1 British Army officers photographed in Kabul, in February 1880, showing the variety of outfits worn while on campaign in Afghanistan.** A number of them are wearing Glengarry caps bearing the badge of the 9th Foot – a numeral 9 surrounded by a garter bearing the words 'East Norfolk Regiment', surmounted by a figure of Britannia carrying a trident, a globe beside her Union Flag shield, her hair in a bun and a lion at her feet. Officers bought their own uniforms and thus most of the jackets and breeches are made by their tailors to a similar pattern but the shades of khaki differ, as do the boots, buskins, stockings and puttees worn; also note some of their hats and gloves are clearly purchased from local bazaars or merchants.

2

**2 Lieutenant Robert Tomkyns Hawkes, Ensign, 7th Foot, Royal Fusiliers, November 1865.** He wears an Undress frock coat with two rows of buttons, practical to his right, decorative to his left. As an Ensign his collar is plain; insignia denoting rank was displayed on the collar. Resting on his thigh is his officer's forage or Undress cap (1852–1881) commonly known as the 'cheese cutter' – the first of a number of military caps to be given this *nom de plume*. These caps were of blue cloth with black lace decorated with oak leaves. Royal regiments wore a scarlet band instead of the lace. In the centre front the cap displays the regimental number; many regiments also surmounted the number with their regimental device either in gold or silver.

**3 Private soldier of 3rd Foot, 'The Buffs' 1861-69.** The photograph can be dated by the 'quilted' shako head-dress. The helmet plate, universal for line infantry, consists of an eight-pointed star, with a Victorian crown obscuring the top point. The centre of the badge bore the regimental number voided in the centre. Above the cap badge, inserted in the front of the crown of the hat is a mounted pom-pom; these were colour coded – two thirds white over one third red for line regiments, white for fusiliers and green for light infantry.

*3*

*4*

**4 Rifleman J. Kennedy, Berkshire Rifle Volunteer Corps 1861-69.** He also wears a 'quilted' shako head-dress. On his cap is a badge bearing the initials of the corps surmounted by a bugle, a familiar device used on many Rifle Volunteer corps' cap badges. The braid or cords around his hat would have been distinctive to his regiment. The shako and his uniform were made from a grey material.

5

**5 A Royal Engineer in full dress, 1855-69.** His fur busby would have had a blue bag hanging down the right side with a brass grenade with white goat's hair plume, dating him to this period; the quality of this photo and the fact that the original is a carte-de-visite from a commercial photographer suggests the later 1860s. Note the stripe in his trousers is a broad one adopted by corps rather than the thin pencil line of the line infantry.

**6 Lieutenant Colman, Norfolk Artillery Militia, c1875.** His rank is denoted by the lace knot on his cuff; a similar style was adopted by all corps. Line infantry officer cuff rank insignia was based around a gold-braided chevron, surmounted by a smaller knot. Increasing numbers of chevrons for line infantry and lace embellishments for both infantry and corps indicated higher ranks. He wears the officer's forage cap introduced in 1870. His cap braid and circular lace around his cap boss clearly denote him as Artillery. The fine set of whiskers he sports certainly dates him to the late 1870s when this style was popular.

6

7

**7 11th Middlesex Rifle Volunteer Corps, c1878.** Sometimes the military units represented on cap badges are not immediately obvious. The symbol of St George and the Dragon is usually associated with the Northumberland Fusiliers but in this case it is the badge of 11th Middlesex Rifle Volunteer Corps, who were formed in the Parish of St George.

**8 Gunners of 2nd Detachment, No.3 Battery, Norfolk Artillery Volunteers, c1881.** They are in shirt sleeve order, a state of dress allowed for energetic work or fatigues. They all wear forage caps otherwise known as 'pill-box hats', worn by corps officers, NCOs and ORs until the 'Broderick cap' was introduced in 1902. NCOs are delineated by chevrons on the front of their hats, volunteer officers had silver braid.

8

9

**9 A Regular Soldier Private, The Suffolk Regiment, c1884.** A typical line infantry soldier after the Cardwell reforms of 1881. He wears an Undress frock jacket with the seven front buttons prescribed for home service, while a five-button pattern was for use in India (although examples of this type can be found worn in the UK). The Glengarry was bound at the bottom with black silk or leather with silk tails (one of the silk tails can be seen behind his left ear).

10

**10 A Regular Soldier Private, The East Surrey Regiment, c1885.** He wears a dress tunic and the home service helmet that had been introduced in 1878. His grey greatcoat has been rolled and the extremities tied or strapped together, and it is worn bandolier-style over his left shoulder. This dress code normally applied when full equipment was not required but the weather looked inclement or duties would require it to be worn, otherwise the coat would be rolled and strapped above the back pack. His 'jam pot' cuffs distinguish him as a soldier from a Regular battalion. He is holding a Martini-Henry Mark III rifle (1879-1888).

*11*

**11 Sergeant Henry Lacey, Drill and Musketry Instructor B Company (Diss), 4th Volunteer Battalion, The Norfolk Regiment, c1895.** He wears the 'full dress' tunic edged with white down the left front like the Regular battalion soldiers (the right front had white edging from waist level to the bottom edge) and, as a senior NCO, has white chevron cuffs trimmed with black lace and Austrian knots. The crossed rifles and crown insignia on his arm denotes he has qualified as a musketry instructor; each white star above the cuff indicates three years' proficient service with good conduct.

*12*

**12 Lieutenant Alec B. Stewart, 3rd Militia Battalion, The King's Own (Yorkshire Light Infantry) in levee dress, c1890.** He wears the home service helmet that had been introduced in 1878 and the twisted gold shoulder cords introduced in 1880. At the bottom of this officer's shoulder board is the letter 'M' which denotes him a member of the Militia battalion.

**13 Lieutenant Colonel, Isle of Wight Rifles, c1890.** His rank insignia of a crown and pip can be discerned on his shoulder braid. His tunic has the distinctive lace and toggles of Rifle regiments and would have been of rifle-green cloth with collar and cuffs in black velvet. His cross-belt badge bears the device of a tower in the centre, unique to the Isle of Wight Rifles; the badge is also surmounted by a Victorian crown. The whistle on the chain provides further confirmation that he is a member of a Rifle regiment.

13

**14 Second Lieutenant Charles Donovan, Royal Artillery, Rawal Pindi, India, February 1884.** To his right is his pith hat. He wears a khaki frock coat cut in the style of the patrol jacket, with pointed pocket flaps and all small regimental buttons. As a Second Lieutenant he has no pips on his epaulettes but has the shoulder title 'RA' for Royal Artillery (distinctive letters or numerals were worn below pips at this time by officers to indicate corps, regiment or department). His left hand rests on the 1821 pattern Royal Artillery officer's sword. He wears riding breeches and knee boots permitted for mounted officers.

14

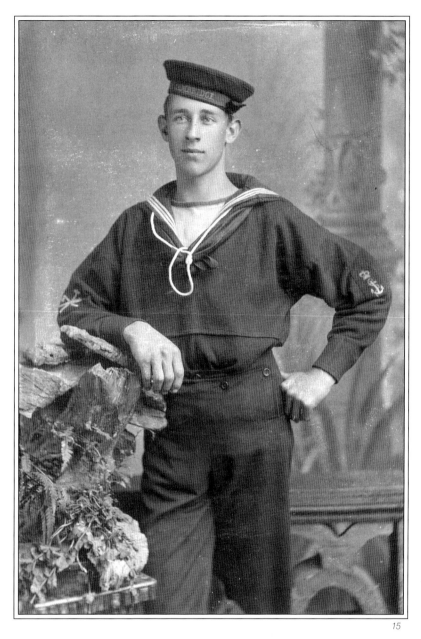

15

**15 Second Class Petty Officer, Royal Navy, c1890.** On his left arm is his 'badge of rating' – a crown and anchor denoting a Second Class Petty Officer. His cap tally states he is serving with HMS *Cambridge*, the famous Naval Gunnery School at Devonport, Plymouth. The 'cross axe and hammer with gun' on his right arm is his trade badge for Armourer's Crew.

16

**16 Second Class Petty Officer, Royal Navy, c1888.** His style of dress shows him as he would have appeared for inspections, musters, ceremonial occasions and on Sundays in harbour. Below his badge of rating is one good conduct badge. On his lower right arm is the cross rifles of his Good Shooting badge (Second Class) and above that the gun and crown of a Gunnery Instructor (who had not been through the torpedo course). His cap tally shows him serving aboard HMS *Imperieuse* (sister ship of HMS *Warspite*), an armoured cruiser that served as flagship on the China Station from 1889-94, and then the Pacific Station 1896-99.

**17 Second Class Stoker, Royal Navy, c1890.** He wears his blue frock, neck handkerchief, square rig and lanyard exactly as per regulations. The three-bladed propeller on his right arm is his trade badge denoting him as a Stoker (Second Class).

17

# The Edwardian Era

## 1901-1913

The South African War (1899-1902) not only exposed weaknesses and inefficiency in the British Army but also the poor literacy, numeracy and, in many cases, health of its volunteers. These problems were particularly addressed in the Esher Report that made a number of recommendations, most notably a brand new approach to the recruit selection process, training and organisation of the British Army.

In 1908 Richard Burdon Haldane, the new Liberal Government's War Secretary, had the duty of implementing the Esher Report's recommendations. With his team of advisers he provided the army with official manuals laying down, in detail, staff responsibilities and procedures in the form of Field Service Regulations. The greatest task was, however, the complete reorganisation of the Home Field Army and Reserve system, which created the Territorial Force from the old Volunteer system, and the provision of the British Expeditionary Force (BEF). The notion being that the regular battalions would provide the garrison troops for the Empire and form a BEF from 'Home' garrisoned troops in the event of a 'war emergency', while it was intended that the Territorial Force should remain at home and defend Britain.

In 1907 there were 221 battalions of Volunteer infantry in England, Scotland and Wales (there were no Volunteers in Ireland at the time). The new scheme saw line infantry regiment battalions given sequential numbers, ie the Regular battalions were the 1st and 2nd, the 3rd became a Militia battalion and the Territorials the 4th and 5th Battalions.

In addition to these reforms, Haldane also saw to it that an Officer Training Corps was formally established to create a 'seed bed' of young officers for the reformed army. Several new units entirely composed of Territorial soldiers were created, namely Monmouthshire, Cambridgeshire, Hertfordshire and Herefordshire Regiments and the many battalions of the London Regiment. There were also eleven much heralded Territorial Force Cyclist battalions allocated to county regiments across Britain.

The requirements to join the Territorials were clearly laid out in the recruitment booklets. Men had to be aged between 17 and 35, with a minimum chest measurement of 33 inches and a minimum height of 5 ft 2 inches, and would have to enlist for a minimum of four years in the Territorial Force. Upon joining, the recruit was obliged to attend 40 drills in his first year. In the battalion, one hour on two days each week was set aside for recruit drill. He was also required to pass through a recruits' course of musketry held on two appointed afternoons through the summer months. Throughout this period there would be regular parades and weekend manoeuvres, which any recruit would find soon earned him the nickname of a 'Saturday Night Soldier'.

This period therefore sees a change in uniform detail for the Volunteers that can be useful for dating purposes (8, 11, 12). Uniform was pretty standard for the English and Welsh Territorials, who were issued with the same khaki serge 'service dress' uniforms of jacket, trousers, stiff top hat and puttees as the regular soldiers, many units asking their Territorial soldiers to provide their own shirts and boots (5). Along with the basic uniform they also had a greatcoat, waterproof cape and a set of the 1908 pattern webbing. Their best parade and 'walking out' dress consisted of a blue stiff cap, red frock tunic and trousers – boots, buttons and badges all well shone, of course. In the case of Scottish regiments the trousers were mostly replaced with kilts, socks, puttees and spats. Tunics frequently had the 'cut away' to the front flaps of the jacket and a variety of Glengarries and tam o'shanters were worn as per regimental distinctions, traditions and orders.

In many instances the cap badge and insignia of the Territorial battalion soldier was subtly different from their Regular battalion counterparts. For example, the Lincolnshire Regiment's plinth under its sphinx is blank, while on the Regulars it bears their battle honour 'Egypt', and the Leicestershire Regiment's tiger has its upper battle honour title of 'Hindoostan' (sic) omitted from the Territorial badge. While on the shoulder titles, where Regulars would normally simply have their county designation in a semi-circle of brass lettering such as 'Norfolk', 'Suffolk' or 'Devon', the Territorials would also have their battalion designation such as 'T 4' Norfolk or 'T 5' Devon etc juxtaposed to the county designation.

Many Territorials also affected the old tradition when 'walking out' of carrying a swagger stick with a silver-coloured top (often 'white metal' or cupro-nickel rather than silver) embossed with the regimental badge or crest. This cane or stick should have always been carried tucked under the left armpit – woe betide any soldier attempting to salute (always given with the right hand) while he had a stick in his palm!

In the second, third and fourth year of service the recruit became a 'Trained Man' and was obliged to perform 20 drills in the second year and 10 drills in the third and fourth years, as well as the Trained Man's Course of Musketry. A unique badge of the Territorial Force was the five-pointed star worn on the right forearm by ORs and NCOs to denote the wearer had been returned as 'qualified' four times. This return was measured over a period of one year and subsequent stars were awarded for every aggregate of four years.

Pay was not bad – a private soldier would draw a shilling a day, a corporal 1s 8d, sergeant 2s 4d, up to colour sergeant on 3s 6d per day, plus an additional 3 shillings for those who attended camp for 'wear and tear of boots'. The members of the cyclist battalions did very well. Each man had to own his own bicycle and his allowance for use of his bike at camp was the grand sum of £1 for eight days and 1s 6d for each subsequent day.

Headgear may vary in photographs of this period. A side hat with button front was introduced from the 1890s for most British regiments, with the exception of the Scots, to replace the Glengarry (1). This could be unfolded to make a type of balaclava helmet.

Volunteers are also seen in soft felt slouch hats (3), based on those worn during the South African War; they were supposed to be replaced by 'Broderick' caps introduced from 1902 but officers and soldiers disliked the 'Brod' cap and many Volunteer units persisted with their slouch hats until service dress caps were introduced from 1905. The correct nomenclature for the Broderick cap (5) was 'Forage Cap, New Pattern', or 'Forage Cap, Universal', and was nicknamed after William St John Fremantle Broderick, Secretary of State for War. By 1907 it is unusual to see the Broderick caps still being worn (6), because in most regiments they had been replaced by dress caps with a peak.

Regular soldiers serving overseas generally wore standard khaki drill or 'full whites' in hot climes such as India (23, 24, 25) – never issued to soldiers on home service. Cloth badges often appear loosely tacked on to whites and khaki drill in photographs, particularly when the soldiers were newly arrived – time was always at a premium and the badges could not be sewn on perfectly from day to day because of the need to regularly wash uniforms. As their sewing skills were practised more regularly many soldiers became far more adept and the badges, although tacked on, look a lot better. Soldiers in later years were very grateful for the invention of the press stud!

The Royal Navy was also forced to confront the modern world post-1900 and was quick off the mark, when in 1903 the Royal Naval Volunteer Reserve was created. A reserve of civilian volunteers, the first divisions were established in London, on the Clyde and the Mersey. Admiralty officials were impressed from the outset that there was an immediate response to their recruitment advertisements from the right kind of men. When the London Division of the RNVR was started there was a large proportion of yachtsmen in the ranks, who could handle a boat in any circumstances and were familiar with the approaches to the capital.

Senior naval officers saw this wind of change as a great opportunity to modernise the Royal Navy and to push for HMS *Dreadnought* – the first all iron-clad, all big-gun, turbine-driven battleship. The Navy also looked to the reform and improvement of its training establishments to keep its officers and ratings in step with such new developments as wireless telegraphy, torpedoes and submarines. The uniforms, and particularly the qualification badges and insignia, reflect the changes for men qualified in these pioneering areas (28). Also look out for badges and insignia delineating pioneers of the newly formed Royal Naval Air Service (from 1912).

*1*

**1 Ryburgh Detachment, 3rd Volunteer Battalion, The Norfolk Volunteers, 1901.** Photographed on 2 February 1901, the day of Queen Victoria's State Funeral, when commemoration services were held in her honour across the country. The men wear the side hat with button front introduced from the 1890s. Most wear tunics with pointed white facings with cord Austrian knots; a feature used to delineate Volunteers from Regular troops since 1881. Two others, however, wear the seven-button serge frock with 'jam pot cuff' sometimes adopted by ex-regular soldiers in the Volunteers; the campaign medal and regular army good conduct stripes confirm this on the ex-regular soldier second from left on the front row.

2

**2 Grenadier Guards Regimental Sergeant Major, c1902.** A soldier truly at the top of his craft. Dressed in Drill Order, he wears the RSM's forage cap, the grenade badge with applied silver crown and Royal cyphers (ORs wore plain brass). He has a 'First Quality' tunic with additional gold lace on the collar and shoulder straps and the distinctive four-button and gold lace hoops above his cuff. His collar badges would have been worked in silver on gold lace. The RSM's sword is worn from his belt and he carries a pace stick. He wears the Guards' unique RSM's badge worked in gold, silver and coloured threads on his right upper arm only. This picture can be dated to 1902 or very shortly afterwards because the most recent medal in his group of four is a King Edward VII Coronation Medal, issued in 1902.

3

**3 3rd Middlesex Rifle Volunteers outside Hackney Drill Hall, 1907.** Their history as a Rifle battalion is marked by the black cross straps, pouches and belt of the valise equipment, 1882 pattern, they are wearing. Their soft felt slouch hats are based on those worn during the South African War.

*4*

**4 Officers of 2nd Battalion, The Lincolnshire Regiment, c.1907.** The dark blue Undress frock coats with crimson sashes can be traced back to the mid-19th century, but the gilded pips on the shoulders, regimental collar badges and smart dark blue caps with shiny peaks date the picture to the first decade of the 20th century. In unattributed photographs such attire is a good indicator that the subjects are Regular army officers rather than Volunteers or (later) Territorials.

**5 Private Soldier, 2nd Volunteer Battalion, The Essex Regiment, c1905.** He wears the Broderick cap, introduced in 1902. The khaki tunic has twisted shoulder cord epaulettes, worn 1904-1907. The cap badge is the Essex Regiment (his shoulder cloth insignia would have read simply 'Essex' in white lettering on red background). The two small cloth insignia below state '2 V', thus denoting him as 2nd Volunteer Battalion; his buttons would bear the standard Royal Arms but would have been in white metal. His valise equipment belt (in dark brown or black because the 2nd VB were Rifle Volunteers) and 'civvy' boots confirm his status.

*5*

6

**6 Other Ranks of the 2nd Battalion, The Lincolnshire Regiment on Duties Parade, c1907.** They wear 'full dress' of scarlet tunics with medals, dark blue trousers with thin red infantry stripe and have their swagger canes tucked under their arms. They are still wearing the unpopular Broderick caps. Again, a good indicator that the subjects are Regular army soldiers rather than Volunteers or (later) Territorials.

**7 Regular Army Bugler, 2nd Battalion, The Lincolnshire Regiment, c1907.** Such 'full dress' uniforms certainly hark back to the army of Queen Victoria, but look closer and the King's crown can be seen to surmount the helmet plate badge and he wears both the Queen's and King's South Africa medals. Above his cuff can be seen a Good-Conduct chevron awarded for two years' 'clean' service record.

7

8

**8 Volunteer Artillery Officers in 'Full Dress', 1909.** Although the helmet plates' crowns are both Victorian, the original photo has a contemporary annotation dating it. It was quite common for Volunteers and even Territorial unit officers to be seen wearing helmet plates with Queen Victoria crowns up to about 1911. The Lieutenant (left) has two pips on his shoulder cords, the Captain three: this is an important dating clue because in 1902 Second Lieutenants were given a single star or 'pip' for the first time, thus full Lieutenants were given an extra star for their rank insignia and Captains were increased from two to three stars. Also note the braid above the cuff, simple for the Lieutenant, increasingly embellished from the rank of Captain and above.

9

**9 Regular Soldiers, Royal Army Medical Corps (left) and Royal Artillery (seated), c1907.** Smartly turned out in blue dress tunics typical of Corps, their shoulders have the twisted cords worn 1904-7 and they wear peaked forage caps. Cap badge, collar grenades and wide stripe on the trousers identify our artilleryman. Our RAMC soldier also has cap badge and collar badges, in his case the laurel, serpent and staff badge of the RAMC, but he also wears the distinctive roundel with a red cross on white background in the centre surrounded by a gold wire or yellow cloth circle and dark navy backing.

**10 Essex Regiment Volunteer Battalion, Regimental Police, c1907.** Armed with sturdy sticks (sometimes pick-axe handles), these would be the men charged with maintaining order and military discipline in their Volunteer battalion. In the Volunteers, RPs are most frequently seen when the troops were in transit, on manoeuvres or at camp. The Sergeant wearing the MP (Military Police) armband is the Provost Sergeant – he is in charge of the Regimental Police and is responsible to the Regimental Sergeant Major – while the three others wear RP (Regimental Police) on their armbands. As a general rule the Provost Sergeant would remain in post but most of the men who acted as RPs would be chosen men and would do this duty on a roster.

10

*11*

**11 B (Dunstable) Company, 5th Battalion, The Bedfordshire Regiment, 1908.** Winners of the Battalion Cup (the gentleman dressed all in black in the centre is the battalion Padre). Photographed very shortly after the change from Volunteers to Territorials, most of these men are still wearing Volunteers' shoulder titles and although they look very smart in their valise pattern equipment, it dated back to the 1880s and was soon scrapped in favour of the 1908 pattern webbing equipment.

**12 Probably a family group of Sergeants and one Private all serving in the Sherwood Foresters (Notts & Derby Regiment) at the time of the Volunteers/Territorials change over in 1908.** Although the shoulder titles are undistinguishable, their size is a clue – Regular battalions would have the title 'Notts & Derby' whereas the Volunteers or Territorials would have either a 'V' or a 'T' and a number to designate their battalion. Their 'full dress' tunics have material epaulettes rather than the twisted cord phased out in 1907, and the Colour Sergeant seated left wears a Volunteers' Long Service Medal. On their right arms are also displayed the service stars worn by Volunteers and Territorials instead of Service 'stripes' before the First World War. The Sergeant seated centre wears a Musketry qualification badge on his left forearm, the older sergeant on the left wears a Volunteers' Musketry Instructor's badge.

*12*

COLOUR PARTY, 1ST HERTS.

13

**13 Colour Party and Escorts, 1st Battalion, The Hertfordshire Regiment (TF), c1910.** The officers are in their blue 'patrols' with white 'tops' on their hats (normally worn as part of dress regulations during the summer), Sam Browne belts and swords. The escorts wear the red tunics with regimental coloured facings. The Colour Sergeant (centre) wears the crossed flags and crown that distinguish his rank above the sergeant's stripes on his right arm. Two of the Sergeants have Territorial Force Long Service medals, distinguishable by the oval shape and single lighter stripe up the centre of the ribbon (in colour the background of the medal ribbon would have been green, the stripe yellow).

14

**14 5th Battalion, The Suffolk Regiment (TF), Sergeants Mess at Camp, c1912.** This group photograph shows these men of a pre-war Territorial Force battalion as a confident and established unit. Some are in khaki ready to give instruction and drill, some (mostly members of the band) are in their scarlet tunics with medals worn, but many are ready for parade wearing the NCOs' and ORs' 'blues' – distinguishable in black and white by the small buttons and breast pockets.

**15 Machine Gun Detachment, Bedfordshire Regiment TF Battalion, c1910.** Hiram Maxim developed his machine gun in the early 1880s and his company was bought by the giant Vickers Armstrong Ltd in 1896. First supplied to the Regular army, Maxim guns were phased in for the new Territorial Force from its creation in 1908 and by 1910 to 1912 most Territorial battalions had developed their Machine Gun Sections. Some members of the General Staff considered the deployment of Maxims cumbersome and more than one was heard to shout 'Get that ******* cart out of the way' during exercises.

15

*16*

**16 Officers of 1st East Anglian Brigade, Royal Field Artillery,
1912.** Like the soldiers' service dress of the period 1902 to 1907, that
worn by officers did fasten up to the neck and twisted cords were worn at
the shoulder. The similarities ended there, the cloth was a good quality
green barathea or a fine wool. At his neck would be Corps or Regimental
collar badges and his rank was displayed just above the cuff. This picture
dates from 1912 when open-neck officers' jackets were widely introduced
for the first time. Still getting used to this new feature, officers did not
always wear a khaki shirt and tie with it in this period.

*17*

**17 Regular Army Battalion Soldiers of The Suffolk Regiment, 'Minden Day', 1 August 1909.** A day celebrated with special parades and events to commemorate the famous victory at Minden on 1 August 1759. The men of the regiments involved – namely 12th Foot (Suffolk Regiment), 20th Foot (Lancashire Fusiliers), 23rd Foot (Royal Welch Fusiliers), 25th Foot (King's Own Scottish Borderers), 37th Foot (Hampshire Regiment), 51st Foot (King's Own Yorkshire Light Infantry) – wore yellow and red 'Minden' roses with their cap badge to mark the occasion. The tunics worn by this group illustrate the change-over period; the soldier, centre left, still has the twisted shoulder cords and 'Suffolk' cloth insignia while the others have the new tunics with epaulettes and brass shoulder titles.

18

**18 NCOs, 1st Volunteer Battalion, The Northamptonshire Regiment, c1908.** Their grey uniforms, black leather cross straps and whistles belie their battalion's origins as 1st Northamptonshire Rifle Volunteer Corps. Three of the men pictured are wearing Queen's South Africa Medals from the time when members of the battalion volunteered and served in the South African War. The Haldane Reforms of 1908 saw the battalion become 4th Battalion, The Northamptonshire Regiment (TF).

*19*

*20*

**19 Soldiers of the Essex Regiment, c1912.** The soldier on the left is wearing the 1903 pattern equipment consisting of a bandolier with five ten-round pockets in front with waist belt and 'pockets cartridge'. Although superseded by the 1908 pattern webbing, the Pattern 1903 was worn by some Territorials, for example, for cycle-mounted duties until the First World War. The bandolier was worn by some mounted and corps troops until the early years of the Second World War.

**20 Sergeant, Lovat's Scouts Yeomanry, c1912.** Even with the introduction of service dress some regiments, especially the Yeomanry, liked to maintain certain dress traditions and distinctions. One of the most unique was the uniform of Lovat's Scouts with buttons above the cuff, collar badges and their own distinctive bonnet.

21

**21 Sergeant, XX Hussars, c1912.** He wears his regimentally tailored service dress which has subtle differences to the issue version, such as exterior pockets and breeches. He is wearing collar badges (an unusual feature to be seen on NCOs' and especially ORs' SD uniforms before and during the First World War) and rather than the standard puttees he wears a smart pair of leather buskins, spurs and boots.

22

**22 Squadron Corporal Major (WO II), Loyal Suffolk Hussars, c1912.** His shoulder title 'TY' Suffolk denotes Territorial Yeomanry. In his hands are a riding crop and a muster roll book and pencil. The use of a whistle instead of bugles to call up the squadron became usual after the LSH's return from the South African War and this SCM shows it with pride – almost as much a badge of office as the stripes and crowns on his arms.

**23 A Regular Army Battalion, Royal Warwickshire Regiment Colour Sergeant and his wife, India, c1905.** Above the Colour Sergeant flags on his arm is clearly an embroidered King's crown. On his chest he wears an India Medal (1895-1902) which, if he was serving there in the period 1899-1902, would explain the absence of at least one South African War medal.

23

24

**24 Private, 2nd Battalion, The Norfolk Regiment, Belgaum, India, 1912.** He wears the full 'whites' with Regimental buttons and collar badges. Properly called 'white uniform', it could only be worn by all men of a battalion under the authority of the General Officer Commanding. His Wolseley helmet has a yellow 'pugaree' with cap badge displayed at the front. Such coloured pugarees were distinctions allowed to only a few English regiments. On his left arm are two good conduct stripes and a marksman qualification badge.

25

**25 Private, 2nd Battalion, The Norfolk Regiment, Belgaum, India, 1912.** He is dressed in 'walking out' order (no webbing, polished boots, pressed uniform and swagger cane in hand) in the standard khaki drill worn for foreign service in hot climes at the time. On the seat beside him is his Wolseley pattern sun helmet. In the absence of visible cap badge or shoulder titles his regiment may be discerned from the 'flash' or ribbon worn around the pugaree.

26

**26 Cadet Roderick McLeod, Royal Military Academy, Woolwich, 1911.** Established in 1741, RMA Woolwich became known as 'the Shop'. The good career prospects and interesting appointments open to military Engineering Officers meant there was always strong competition to be selected and it was very much in the interest of gentleman cadets to study for their commissions in the Royal Engineers and Artillery. The RMA, Woolwich, closed in 1939. Roderick McLeod served with distinction during the First World War, he was decorated with the Military Cross and the Distinguished Service Order and retired a Colonel in the Royal Artillery.

**27 Commander, Royal Navy, 1903.** He is photographed in 'Full Dress' uniform with bicorn hat and sword, a form of dress reserved only for full ceremonial occasions. On his chest are ribbons for the Egypt Medal instituted in October 1882 for the Egyptian campaign of the same year and extended to include the later Egyptian campaigns, up to 1889. Beside that is the ribbon of the Khedive's Star awarded to all who qualified for the Egypt Medal.

27

*28*

**28 Wireless Telegraphist 2nd Class, Royal Navy, c1910.** His uniform with waistcoat and fold-away tie date this picture before the First World War, and when wireless telegraphy was something new to the Royal Navy. The first five RN wireless sets were installed on the cruisers HMS *Dwarf, Forte, Magicienne, Racoon* and *Thetis* in 1900 and badges for wireless telegraphists were only adopted in 1909 and worn on the collar. He is wearing the Royal Navy LS&GC (with Edward VII obverse), which represents 15 years' Long Service and Good Conduct. Considering his length of service and the rank he had achieved at the time of this photograph, it is feasible that this gentleman was among the Royal Navy's first wireless telegraphists.

**29 Able Seaman, Royal Navy, c1910.** His cap tally reads: 'Steam Launch No.122'. Royal Navy steam launches were used for a number of purposes such as running personnel from ship to ship, transfer of supplies to reconnaissance and the transportation of raiding parties.

# The First World War
## 1914-1918

The First World War saw some of the most dramatic developments in the entire history of the British forces, from the recruitment of entire new armies to the creation of uniformed military units for women, to the use of aerial warfare and the development of tanks. All of these features can be seen to be reflected in and observed from the badges, insignia and uniforms of our ancestors in the First World War.

The structure of the British Army in 1914 can be divided into three main categories. The first, the Regular Army, comprised four regiments of Foot Guards; 69 line infantry regiments; three Household and 25 Cavalry regiments of the line plus Corps troops such as Artillery, Engineers and Medical. The British Army consisted of 125,000 professional officers, NCOs (non-commissioned officers) and soldiers. Every line infantry soldier in the Regular Army would have volunteered and 'signed on the dotted line' for, at least, the minimum term of seven years 'with the colours', with five on the Reserve. After the Haldane Reforms of 1908 (see Chapter 2) it was also from the Regular Army that a British Expeditionary Force (BEF) would be formed and dispatched post haste in the event of a European emergency.

Those who had left the army but were retained on the Reserve could be called up to bring the Regular Army up to full strength. Reservists were classified into four categories: 'A' – those who could be immediately called for any minor emergency (for which they were also paid a premium); 'B' – the general reserve; 'C' – general service men transferred prematurely; and 'D' – men whose time on the Reserve had expired but who volunteered to remain on call for another four years. Alongside them were the Special Reserve, previously known as 'militia men', who had volunteered to keep their names on the Reserve.

The final category, as we have seen, was the Territorial Force, a totally separate volunteer army of part-time soldiers. When the winds of war blew in 1914 the War Office knew that Territorial soldiers were under no obligation to fight overseas, but knowing the 'call may come' a general appeal was put out to the Territorial battalions for volunteers for overseas service. The response was very positive, with many Territorial battalions sending in returns of around 90% volunteering 'to do their bit overseas'. A white metal pin-backed badge bearing the legend 'Imperial Service' surmounted by a crown was issued to those who so volunteered before 30 September 1914, and was worn with great pride above the right pocket on the tunic (29). This badge tends not to be seen worn from mid-1915 and even though they also had to volunteer to serve abroad, many TF officers chose not to wear it.

Very few Territorial units were to see action in the opening battles of the First World War like Mons or the Marne. In fact most were tasked with the duties for which they were originally raised – guarding the homeland. Many of the Territorial cyclist battalions were deployed in patrolling and maintaining coastal defences, thus providing the 'first line' in the event of an invasion (16, 29). But as the war widened, many Territorials went to France and Flanders and provided major quotas for the campaigns in Gallipoli and in the Middle East.

War was declared at 11 pm on 4 August 1914, and the next day Field Marshal Earl Kitchener was formally appointed Secretary of State for War. For the people of Britain it appeared a wise choice. Kitchener, or 'K of K' (Kitchener of Khartoum), as he was often known, was a national hero who had come to prominence during the colonial small wars of the latter half of the 19th century, notably at the legendary Battle of Omdurman. He was one of the few senior officers far-sighted enough to see the war was certainly not going to be over by Christmas and that to have sufficient numbers of trained soldiers to fight for Britain, he would have to step up the recruitment campaign.

Because of his foresight, and perhaps not some small amount of jealousy, Kitchener was not a popular appointment with some of the senior Regular Army staff officers, who proved awkward and in some cases deliberately obstructive to his plans. Kitchener also found the Territorial Force 'unwieldy'. He had been opposed to its creation in 1908 and was not prepared to use its framework for his expansion plans. Kitchener wanted completely new armies, malleable and untainted by old military doggerel. In every way they would be 'Kitchener's Armies' and the soldiers would proudly say they were 'Kitchener Men'. On the same day that he formally assumed his duties, Kitchener presented his request for another 500,000 men to Parliament. He believed the country should prepare itself for at least three years of conflict that would require some 70 Divisions to fight it. The men he would wish to call upon would all be volunteers, each enlisting as a regular soldier for three years or the duration of the war, who would also commit to serve anywhere, home or abroad.

On 11 August 1914 Kitchener's famous call to arms – Your King and Country Need You – was first published, calling for 100,000 men between the ages of 19 and 30 to enlist; ex-soldiers were accepted up to the age of 45. The appeal was met with widespread patriotic zeal. Men fiddled their birth certificates at both ends of the scale to enlist. A tale familiar to most parts of the country tells of young, well built lads presenting themselves to Recruiting Sergeants; at interview they would be asked their age, some said 16, the old Sergeant would weigh the lad up, if he looked sizeable to pass muster he would be told to 'go out, come back in and tell me different.' Outside the door would no doubt be a few chaps in uniform who would 'put the boy right', he would return, tell the Sergeant he was 19 and he would be signed up for active service.

By 21 August Kitchener had received his first hundred thousand recruits and what became known as 'K1', the first six divisions of the 'New Army', was approved by the War Office. In total there were to be five 'New Armies' formed under the Kitchener scheme, and this meant most line infantry regiments received about three battalions of the new army (some, such as the Middlesex or the Manchester Regiment had many more). Carrying on regimental numbering, the typical county regiment would have the following active service battalions: 1st and 2nd Battalions (Regular Army troops), 4th, 5th and 6th Battalions (Territorials), and 7th, 8th and 9th (Service) Battalions provided by 'Kitchener' men.

At this point it is worth exploring the command structure of an Infantry Division in the First World War. Most Infantry Divisions would be led by a Lieutenant General or Major-General and would contain a mix of corps and infantry personnel with total strength of about 598 officers and 18,077 NCOs and men. Within the Division there would be normally three brigades, under the command of a Brigadier-General; brigades were made up of four battalions of line infantry with 800-1,000 men in each battalion. Each battalion was headed by the OC (Officer Commanding), normally a Lieutenant-Colonel, and comprised HQ Company (OC, adjutant, clerks, quartermaster, signallers, drivers etc) and then four rifle companies, normally named 'A', 'B', 'C' and 'D', each commanded by a Major (or Captains, Lieutenants and Second Lieutenants depending on casualties). Each rifle company consisted of 240 NCOs and men, each divided into four platoons of 60 men. Infantry platoons were then divided into sections led by an NCO (a Sergeant, Corporal or Lance Corporal, again depending on casualties).

By September 1914 an average of 33,000 recruits were enlisting into the forces on a daily basis. As far as supplies went, officers were fortunate. Although they had to buy their own uniform and personal equipment (5), there were plenty of local tailors and national companies such as the Army & Navy Stores who had bolts of green serge, barathea and similar quality cloth in various shades of khaki and green to supply the needs of newly enlisted subalterns (3, 4, 5, 6, 7, 8). The full uniform and kit for officers was expensive and precluded some men from obtaining a commission in the early years of the war and they entered military service as 'gentleman rankers' (34), typically joining regular cavalry and local yeomanry units. In later war years demand was such that more suppliers concentrated on officers' kit and it became more affordable.

Initially hats were stiffened by wire (3), but once officers and men got in the field they removed the stiffeners from the tops of their hats for comfort, greater practicality and to make them less recognisable to the enemy; a look soon adopted by newly commissioned officers in Britain before they left for the front so they did not look so 'green' (9, 13). Swords, too, were seldom seen in later war studio photographs when the nature of warfare had changed to the degree that swords were seen as very old fashioned in the 'modern army' (3, 9).

At the front some officers put away their Service Dress and dressed almost exactly like the men, even going so far as to wear their webbing. Officers were then identified by their own troops by the likes of white triangles sewn onto the backs of the tunics before they led an attack. Some officers, however, persisted in wearing their cuff rank tunics; it was a personal choice, not army regulation of shoulder or cuff insignia, until 1920 when cuff ranks were finally abolished.

For the newly enlisted men who were issued their uniforms and equipment, supplies rapidly became piecemeal. Poor old Quartermasters were often seen red faced and frustratedly scratching their heads after the weekly delivery of odd items of uniform: jackets for three men, caps for five, puttees for ten etc and assorted items of webbing equipment such as a crate of 50 pouches but no belts or cross-straps to attach them to. Factories were at maximum output, most took on more staff and worked shifts around the clock.

A new type of webbing equipment made simply in leather with brass fittings was brought in as an emergency measure in 1914, and by 1915 tunics were being made without details such as pleats in the pockets, but still the supplies could not meet demand (26).

For these men the lack of uniform did not stop their basic training and, told to wear their working clothes (38, 39), they were put through their paces in drill, rifle training and physical exercise, although requests were made for compensation for wear and tear of privately owned clothes and especially boots. Even things as basic as knife, fork and spoon sets had to be shared. A stop-gap for the dearth of uniforms was found by issuing armbands and cap badges to be worn in the lapel of the jacket (some areas even struck their own unofficial badges), but the main drive was to provide some sort of uniform.

Out of desperation the War Office introduced the 'Kitchener Blue', probably the most disliked uniform in the history of the British Army (41, 42). The jackets and trousers were sourced from pre-war uniform stocks held for postmen, prison warders and prisoners. The uniforms for prisoners tended to be grey and had to be dyed for army use.

The army looked to its stores and found its only major stockpile of equipment was the pre-1900 Slade-Wallace and Valise pattern (the classic whitened hide pouches, belts and cross straps worn during the reign of Queen Victoria). The trouble was, the soldiers did not have the pipe clay to re-whiten their grubby old equipment; mind you, there wasn't much of it to go around so most men ended up wearing a belt and one ammunition pouch. This Victorian webbing was accompanied with an issue of rifles of similar vintage, and when these ran out the men were issued with wooden 'dummy' rifles and even broomsticks to practice their drill. The uniform was crowned with a side cap of simple construction.

The public didn't know what to make of these strange blue uniforms and comments were made that 'prison warders' had been conscripted to maintain order; some even thought they were Belgian refugee soldiers. There were still not enough military buttons and regimental badges to go around and even when khaki uniforms became more plentiful, men still ended up wearing collar badges or even buttons in their hats in place of a cap badge. To top it all, much of the dyeing of the uniforms had been done in haste and the dyes ran if the uniform got wet or sweaty, turning the soldier's skin blue.

In typical good humour, the Service Battalion soldiers invented their own song about their tribulations featuring Fred Karno, who was in those days 'King of the Comedians'. There are various versions, this is the cleanest:

> We are Fred Karno's Army,
> Fred Karno's infantry,
> We cannot fight, we cannot shoot,
> What God damn use are we?

But when we get to Berlin,
The Kaiser he will say,
Hoch, Hoch, Mein Gott!
What a bloody fine lot,
Fred Karno's sent today!

The last of the five 'New Armies' was formed under authorization in March 1915. The backbones of the fourth and fifth new armies were to be the groups of soldiers raised in cities and large towns, many of them from the industrial North, known unofficially as 'Pals' or 'Chums' battalions (38).

From May 1915 the 'Kitchener Battalions' proceeded to France and Flanders. Training in trench warfare under battle conditions began when they arrived. Each unit would spend about a month in training. Under the supervision of bawling sergeant instructors the men charged their sacks of hay hung from gallows and stuck their bayonets in key points marked on the bag, fired at targets with the faces of German soldiers printed on them, and some took on specialities such as sniping, advanced signalling, trench mortars and grenade 'bombing'. They were all expected to train in digging and maintaining trenches under fire.

Conscription was not introduced in Britain until January 1916. Lord Derby was appointed Director-General of Recruiting in October 1915 and introduced the 'Derby Scheme' within days of his appointment (40). Men aged 18 to 40 were told that they could continue to enlist voluntarily, or attest with an obligation to come if called up. The War Office notified the public that voluntary enlistment would soon cease and that the last day of registration would be 15 December 1915.

By the end of 1915 there were thirty New Army Divisions in France, three in Macedonia, one in Egypt and two in Gallipoli, with five still training in England. For the boys in France, they were to experience a number of minor battles but suffered heavy casualties. The battalions, however, stood firm through the freezing winter of 1915 into the spring of 1916. The French were being hammered at Verdun and the 'Big Push' was set for 1 July 1916, a day which will be forever marked as the First Day of the Battle of the Somme.

For many Kitchener men, they felt this was it, this is what they had trained and fought for, one last big push. They went bravely 'over the top' into a hail of German bullets. The events, the bravery and the sacrifice of that first day are legendary. Some 60,000 soldiers were killed, maimed, and wounded, but the Battle went on until 18 November. A total of some 420,000 British casualties were sustained in the Somme battles, and no small part of this number were the men of Kitchener's Armies. Many of those who had volunteered together, served together (as per a promise made to the volunteers under the Lord Derby scheme), especially those who made up the 'Pals' battalions. In the staccato fire of enfilading machine guns and amid shot and shell, large numbers of men from very localized areas fell together. The effect of such losses on their home towns and villages was profound.

Add to the carnage on the Somme the casualties of the Royal Navy, Army and Royal Air Force serving in theatres all over the world and it is hardly surprising that by 1918 there was talk of the 'loss of a generation'. Such was the demand for mourning black that many bereaved widows had to make do with armbands. Everyone seemed to be related to or to know someone among the fallen.

Many myths and family legends arose on the front, including that a bible could stop a bullet (61). In fact there are numerous instances of not only bibles but also Princess Mary gift tins and even clips of ammunition carried in the webbing stopping bullets, and I have met a number of families who still cherish such relics as the item 'that saved Grandad's life'. Although it must be said, on balance, that a direct shot within range would probably not have been stopped by any of the above, but had it been slowed by ricochet or great distance a bible may well have stopped a bullet or a piece of shrapnel.

Some photographs may have been taken 'at the front', or more likely in a village or town just behind the lines in a portable daylight photographic studio – in other words, a wooden floor to lift the client out of the mud, basic chair or stool to sit on, and a canvas backdrop probably pinned to a wall (51, 55).

Headgear may give clues to dating. The 'Gorblimey' was introduced in 1915 as a cap designed to combine practicality and warmth (19) – so named after the exultation given by many Sergeant Majors upon seeing this headgear for the first time. The early examples tend to have leather straps or fabric ties, later versions had neither and relied on the fabric-retaining slides that held the flaps on the top of the cap. Although superseded by the soft version of the SD cap in 1917 (20), the 'Gorblimey' can be seen being worn until the end of the war. Shrapnel helmets were first issued in late 1915 (52). This protective headgear, designed to prevent injury from falling shrapnel (it would not stop a bullet unless it had been subject to, perhaps, a ricochet that slowed it down significantly), was also known by a number of names including 'Brodie' (after John L. Brodie who patented the design for these helmets in 1915), 'Tommy' or 'Tin' helmet. Initially there were not enough helmets produced to equip every man so they were designated 'trench stores' and kept at the front line for use by each unit that occupied the sector. It was not until the summer of 1916, when the first one million helmets had been produced, that they were made general issue.

The long greatcoats of 1914 and 1915 (62) caught in the mud in the trenches and it clung to the cloth, weighing them down. They proved so impractical that fur or leather jerkins were introduced (50); some soldiers even took to cutting down their coats to stop them trailing in the mud. By 1915/16 many officers were purchasing 'warms', short double-breasted coats (12), and a shorter greatcoat was issued soon after (63).

Although there had been alterations to the rules in the years before the First World War, between the years 1914-18, as a general rule, Good-Conduct badges (also referred to as 'chevrons' or 'stripes') were earned at a rate of one for each period of 2, 5, 12, 18, 23 and 28 years' service. Soldiers with no significant record of bad behaviour could still have to wait 16, 21 and 26 years for their later badges. Officially, the highest ranks or appointments that could wear Good-Conduct badges were those below full corporal or equivalent (28).

Following a number of incidents in the early war years where discharged service personnel who did not have immediately visible wounds or conditions were taunted as cowards by those who thought they were evading military service, a distinctive Silver War Badge was authorised in September 1916 (74, 75). Any soldier, regardless of whether they had served at home or abroad, who had been given an honourable discharge was entitled to the badge. So if you find one of these badges among family effects do not immediately assume that there are medals to go with it – your ancestor may just have been on home service. Each badge had its own unique number on the reverse – not the man's service number, but the badge number which could be tallied with the entitlement card issued with the badge. The recipients of these badges are frequently referred to as 'Silver Badge Men' in press accounts of parades and events at the end of the war.

Scottish field service dress had many differences to that of English and Welsh regiments. Officers and men did not wear peaked caps but a mix of tam o'shanters (46), bonnets (47) and Glengarries (10, 45). The tam o'shanter was named after the character of that name in the poem by Robert Burns. The bonnet was made of wool, the crown about twice the diameter of the head with a *toorie* (pompom) in the centre. Tunics, properly referred to as doublets, had a cut-away front and kilts were worn with sporrans. In the early years officers and men were also seen at home and on the Western Front wearing Highland shoes, spats and diced hose tops (10, 11, 45, 49). Not every Scottish infantry battalion was kilted, however (49).

For the Royal Navy, it is the cap tally that is often of most help in photographic research (76, 77, 78), the frocks, square rigs and sea jerseys remaining standard from the earlier period. Compared to the Second World War, RN officers' uniforms (81, 82) tended to have a slightly higher-cut open collar. Rounded and winged detachable collars, as well as narrow crowns and small peaks on caps, are also good indicators of early 20th century vintage.

The colour of distinction cloth backings (82) could be of help to distinguish one ancestor from another (though sadly, black and white photographs make this even more difficult): Engineer Officers – purple; Medical Officers – scarlet; Dental Officers – orange; Accountant Officers – white; Instruction Officers and School Masters – light blue; Shipwright Officers – silver grey; Wardmasters – maroon; Electrical Officers – dark green; Ordnance Officers – dark blue.

The Royal Naval Volunteer Reserve founded in 1903 had some excellent commanding officers and real enthusiasts in the ranks, so that when war broke out in 1914 the strength was more than 4,000 officers and men, and the individual quality was markedly high. It was the wavy bands on their square rig, and the cuff lace of RNVR officers, that gave them the nickname of the 'wavy navy' (83).

The Royal Air Force was formed on 1 April 1918 from an amalgamation of the Royal Flying Corps (RFC) and the Royal Naval Air Service (RNAS). The RNAS served both at home and abroad. It had a number of airfields across the country and operated not only with aeroplanes, but also airships. Its main tasks were fleet reconnaissance patrols, scouting and engaging enemy shipping, submarines or airships and conducting offensive raids on enemy coastal territory. The main difference between RNAS uniforms and those of the Royal Navy was the eagle device on their insignia (84, 85, 86).

The uniform of RFC officers was a distinctive side hat, 'maternity' jacket and breeches, with insignia of the letter 'RFC' surrounded by a wreath, surmounted by a King's crown (87, 88). Officers who volunteered for the RFC from regiments or corps were often identified by their parent regiment buttons and badges, but with the addition of RFC wings. They would still remain on the payroll of their regiment but would be officially attached, thus their designation would be, for instance, 'Second Lieutenant J.A. Smith, The Bedfordshire Regiment att. Royal Flying Corps' (88).

Officers' uniforms in the new RAF were originally pale blue (89). One story has it that the pale blue was adopted because the cloth had become available in good quantity and at low cost after its original intended use by the Imperial Russian Cavalry had been curtailed by the Bolshevik Revolution. Folklore or not, this strange, pale stone blue material proved very unpopular. On 15 September 1919, Air Ministry Order 1049 replaced it with the blue-grey colour which has remained in use to this day. Khaki uniform continued to be worn by ORs in the RAF until 1924 when it was replaced by a uniform of blue-grey colour (86, 91, 92).

In the early months a new system of rank insignia was adopted, with bars either side of the cap badge (90). Lieutenants or Second Lieutenants wore one bar; Captains wore two bars. Field Officers wore a single row of gold oak leaves on the cap visor while General Officers wore two. A Second Lieutenant would also wear an eagle on the cuff, without any lace. The higher ranks were indicated by a series of lace bands:

Lieutenant = one broad (2¼ inches) band;
Captain = two standard (½ inch) bands;
Major = two standard bands with a narrow (¼ inch) band in between;
Lt Colonel = three standard bands;
Colonel = four standard bands;
Brigadier General = one broad band;
Major General = one broad and one standard band;
Lieutenant General = one broad and two standard bands;
General = one broad and three standard bands.

Army ranks were used for the RAF from 1 April 1918 until 27 July 1919 when they were replaced by the now familiar RAF ranks.

Few realise that soon after the declaration of war in August 1914 there was a great fear of invasion and out of that fear a form of Home Guard was created during the First World War. Established in 1914, they were known as the Volunteer Training Corps (VTC). Their initial duties saw the men guarding utilities, bridges and key points from attacks by spies, with a motley collection of weaponry (93). On 19 November 1914 the War Office officially recognized the new 'corps' and placed the raised units under the control of the Central Association of Volunteer Training Corps in England and Wales. A similar system was also established in Scotland. Joining regulations were clear; membership was restricted to 'able' men over 38 years of age (the limit was later raised by the War Office to 41) who were not eligible for service in the Regular or Territorial Forces.

Uniforms were eventually sanctioned for the VTC in 1915 on the understanding that they should not look like those worn by the Regular or Territorial army units, so Volunteer uniforms, although of a similar cut, were grey-green in colour (94, 95). And there were quite some variations because they were made by a variety of suppliers, some local, some not and often without clear style directives: made with high collars or low collars, pleated pockets or false pleat pockets, cloth belt fastening etc. If you have a photo of your local unit on parade, look closely and see if they have a number of subtle differences between uniforms. Officers' rank insignia was displayed on the cuff in rings and knots.

After compulsory enlistment began in January 1916, men of suitable service age but found unfit for active service abroad would often be given a choice of being placed with home garrison units or of remaining at home on the condition they joined their local Volunteers. In October 1916 army rank badges were adopted and in December of that same year the first army khaki uniforms were issued to the Volunteers. In July 1918 (with the exception of the units in the City and County of London) they became Volunteer Battalions of their local line regiments. They were permitted to wear their county regiment badges but with no battle honours (100). In most areas it appears it was unusual for the other ranks of the Volunteer units to wear these badges, instead they wore 'General List' badges (Royal Arms supported by the lion and unicorn) (99). Officers often adopted the county cap and collar badges with a letter 'V' beneath; a pattern repeated by other ranks who would wear a 'V' above their county designation shoulder titles on their epaulettes.

Many British subjects had emigrated to Australia, Canada and other parts of the Empire in the years before the First World War, so don't be surprised if you find a photograph of an Australian Imperial Force soldier (for instance) among your family photographs (15, 102). Many romances, too, blossomed while the colourful Aussie soldiers were in Britain and a number of marriages ensued (101).

If you discover a photo of one of your female ancestors in uniform proceed with caution; there was quite a vogue for ladies to be 'daring' and have their photographs taken in their husband's or male relative's uniform, a trend almost certainly started by the popular music hall male impersonator Miss Vesta Tilley (103).

Women were, however, beginning to take their place in the armed services. The Women's Legion (105) was originally proposed in 1915 by Lady Londonderry, as a voluntary service, to meet the shortage of cooks and clerks in the British Army in Britain. They were also employed on other duties but despite being uniformed were not militaristic and did not practise drill. When the Women's Auxiliary Army Corps (WAAC) was formed in 1917 the cooking and general service sections enrolled into it, while the Women's Legion motor transport service, which had been officially used by the British Army from February 1917, carried on until 1919. The drivers wore a claret-coloured patch at the rear of the badge. The volunteers of the Women's Legion were undoubtedly a decisive factor influencing the Government to organise female labour in the latter half of the war.

Women also served in the Army Canteen Committee, created on 1 January 1917 to take over canteens in Great Britain (104). Later retitled the Navy and Army Canteen Board, this organisation took over the Expeditionary Force Canteens in 1919 and formed the nucleus of the NAAFI in 1921.

The Women's Forage Corps (106, 111) was formed by a government initiative in 1915 and was administered by the Army Service Corps, hence most officers and some of the workers wore Army Service Corps cap badges up to about 1917 when their own badge, similar to that of the ASC was introduced. Many Forage Corps officers had large areas to regulate, supplying the army with forage for their horses, and were often found wearing breeches under their skirts so they could ride a motorbike.

Raised in 1917 under the control of the War Office, the Women's Auxiliary Army Corps rapidly enrolled some 57,000 volunteers. The first WAACs proceeded to France on 31 March 1917, and by early 1918 some 6,000 WAACs were there. The organisation was officially renamed Queen Mary's Auxiliary Army Corps (QMAAC) in April 1918, when new cap badges were struck, the main difference being they were headed by a scroll stating 'Queen Mary's', but this title was not generally adopted and the WAACs proudly stayed WAACs. The WAAC was run on military lines; the officers were called Controllers and Administrators, NCOs Forewomen and the equivalent of a private a Worker.

Also created in 1917, the first Wrens of the Women's Royal Naval Service (110) to appear in uniform were enrolled at the RN Depot, Crystal Palace in 1918. Most Wrens were given a trade category – cooks were among the first, soon followed by clerks, wireless telegraphists and electricians – and worked on shore bases or Royal Naval Air Service stations. The Women's Royal Air Force (WRAF) was formed in 1918; it was run, and the women performed duties, along similar lines to the WAAC and WRNS.

**1 & 2 A soldier of the King's Own Royal Regiment Lancaster demonstrates the correct assembly and wear of the 1908 Pattern webbing in 'Full Marching Order' c1919.** The 1908 Pattern webbing was typically used in the years immediately leading up to and during the First World War: the British Expeditionary Force marched to war in 1914 wearing this kit. It comprised a 3 inch wide belt, left and right ammunition pouches which held 75 rounds (in clips of 5 rounds) in each, left and right braces, a bayonet frog with attachment for the entrenching tool handle, water bottle carrier, an entrenching tool head in web cover, small haversack and large pack. Mess tins in khaki covers were worn attached to one of the packs.

Inside the haversack were personal items, knife, fork and spoon, 'housewife' (sewing kit) and the necessities for washing and shaving. The large pack could also be used to stow some of these items, but was usually reserved for carrying the soldier's greatcoat and/or blanket. The original version of this kit had snap-button ammunition pouches but trench warfare soon showed these to be impractical as the pouch flaps became unsnapped by contact with the sides of trenches and valuable, clean ammunition would spill out and fall into the mud. The Army was quick to react and subsequent sets were manufactured with the modified webbing seen here, with strap and stud fastening over the left-hand pockets.

A correctly packed full set of 1908 webbing would weigh 70lbs (32kg), but if it was worn correctly the weight would be evenly distributed. Within reason, it was comfortable to wear, easy to maintain and easily adapted, so it is hardly surprising it lasted for so many years after the Great War and was even used by some units during the early years of the Second World War.

**3  Second Lieutenant, The Norfolk Regiment, 1914.** This is a typical photograph of a newly commissioned officer taken during the very early months of the First World War. His hat has a crown stiffened by wire and a bronze cap badge. His uniform would have had regimental buttons and still has a 'new' look to it, certainly showing little sign of having being worn on the training field, never mind on active service; he is due a quiet word from a friendly brother officer too, to tell him he has got his collar badges facing the wrong way. Like so many newly commissioned officers he proudly wears his sword. As a junior officer, especially in line infantry battalions, be it Regular or Territorial Force, he wears puttees rather than the riding boots worn by some captains, majors and more senior officers.

3

**4 Advert for a military outfitters, 1915.** Every city and many large towns had outfitters and tailors capable of making officers' uniforms, and it was also possible to buy all necessities of uniform, kit and equipment by mail order from the likes of Hyam & Co, Army & Navy Stores and Maxims.

**5 Captain, The King's Own Royal Regiment Norfolk Yeomanry in full Field Kit, 1914.** He is wearing the officer's trench cap; in front of him the flat, square case is his map case which would also have loops for pencils to mark maps, make notes etc. The small leather pouch on the belt was for ammunition; the canvas bag with strap worn over the right shoulder and slung to his left side is his officer's knapsack or side pack used for basic washing kit, rations and similar essentials when in the field. The uppermost leather strap worn across his chest was for binoculars; the case is tucked toward his back behind his left arm. In practice the sword would not have been worn in the field and the map case was worn from clips on the Sam Browne belt or slung by the strap in its place.

**6 Brevet Colonel Sir Horace George Proctor-Beauchamp, 5th Battalion, The Norfolk Regiment, November 1914.** Immaculately turned out, the Colonel would have had a batman – a soldier servant from the ranks of the battalion – to press his uniform and polish his buttons, Sam Browne belt and boots. Beneath each of his Norfolk Regiment collar badges there is a small letter 'T' to denote an officer serving in the Territorial Force.

6

5

**7 Captain, The Manchester Regiment, c1914/15.** He is an older soldier, probably recalled from the Reserve to serve in one of over 40 battalions in the Manchester Regiment that existed during the First World War. His Sam Browne belt has seen a lot of wear and polish but his buttons are leather rather than brass.

7

**8 Lieutenant, Scots Guards, c1915.** Unlike all other British line infantry officers, when in field service dress Guards officers wore their rank insignia upon their shoulders and even had their own regimental pips, but no collar badges and no pleats in their pockets. The ribbons he is wearing show him to have served in the Boer War and that he has been decorated with the Military Cross (instituted 1914). The Coldstream, Scots and Irish Guards officers had well made silver, gilt and enamel cap badges. All Guards officers have caps with polished peaks bound with gold wire. With the exception of the oldest of all the Guards battalions (the Grenadiers), rather than being evenly spaced, Guards buttons are grouped: Coldstreams in twos, Scots in threes as seen here, Irish in fours and Welsh (formed 1915) in groups of five.

9

**9 Second Lieutenant, The Hampshire Regiment, c1915.** This newly commissioned officer is wearing a smartly pressed cuff rank tunic typical of the period, but note he does not wear a sword and the stiffening wire has been taken out of his hat.

**10 Captain, Seaforth Highlanders, c1914.** Scottish Field Service dress was very different to that of English and Welsh regiments, including tunics (doublets) with a 'cut-away' front, cuff ranks sewn with the sweep of the gauntlet cuff and kilts worn with sporrans, Highland shoes, spats and diced hose tops.

*10*

*11*

**11 Second Lieutenant, Gordon Highlanders, c1914/15.**
Smartly turned out, our young Lieutenant shows the Highland
regiments at the front soon learnt it was advisable to protect
their kilts and began wearing a sturdy waterproof khaki apron
with a pocket sewn on the front in place of the sporran.

12

**12 Second Lieutenant, York and Lancaster Regiment, c1917.** He shows what the British army had learned from the conditions on the Western Front. Conditions were too cold for just the waterproof macintosh so the 'officer's warm' he is wearing became very popular in the trenches, though not every officer had one; they were expensive – usually over £2 to buy. He also protects the top of his cap with a waterproof cover.

**13 Lieutenant, South Wales Borderers, c1916.** His hat has had the wire removed and appears 'shaped' and could indicate he has been to the front. His cloth pips also show the trend from 1915 to remove cuff rank insignia after it was proving to be an easy identifier for enemy snipers. The enemy would also be able to identify officers in an attack, thus cloth pips were sewn on the epaulettes.

13

14

**14 Second Lieutenant, South Staffordshire Regiment, 1918.**
Typical of a line infantry officer in walking out order, probably taken
while at rest camp away from the front line – he has gone to a local
town and found a photographer. He wears his trench cap and Sam
Browne belt. His pockets are crammed with the likes of wallet, watch,
cigarette case or pipe and goods bought while on his visit, his batman
has even given his boots a good shine.

**15 Three Australian Officers, France, November 1916.** This delightfully annotated photograph demonstrates that although very similar to British Army uniforms, some Australian army officers wear their caps in their own distinctive way. Australian (AIF) units began to arrive in France from April 1916 and such officers as seen here may well have already served in action at Pozières and what was to prove the worst day of the war for the AIF, at the Battle of Fromelles on 19 July 1916.

15

16

**16 Private, 2nd/7th (Cyclist) Battalion, The Welsh Regiment (TF), 1916.** His mount is one of the 'new government bicycles' supplied to the battalion in 1914, has front and back carriers, and both soldier and cycle are kitted out in 'marching order' as per the specification for military cyclists. His bronzed cap badge, shoulder titles and black rifles buttons reveal the origins of the 7th Battalion as Rifle Volunteers. The Norfolk photographer's name printed on the back of this photo is a clue to the exact battalion: the 1st/7th Battalion never came to Norfolk but the 2nd/7th were in the county 1916-18.

17

**17 Private, The Cambridgeshire Regiment, c1914.** He wears the cap badge showing the Castle of Cambridge superimposed with the Arms of Ely. The main scroll reads 'The Cambridgeshire Regiment', with a scroll beneath bearing the Battle Honour 'South Africa 1900-01'. On his shoulder is the title 'Cambridgeshire' with the letter 'T' above but no number below – because the Cambridgeshires were entirely a Territorial Regiment.

18

**18 Driver, Royal Engineers, c1916.** His cap badge and shoulder title clearly show he serves with the Royal Engineers; he wears the 1903 bandolier familiar to both Artillery and Engineers but his breeches, puttees worn from knee to ankle, and spurs indicate he is part of a mounted unit. On his left forearm is a good conduct stripe.

**19 Lance Corporal, East Lancashire Regiment, c1915.** He wears the unofficial headgear known as a 'Gorblimey' cap introduced in 1915. Superseded by the officially issued soft version of the SD cap in 1917, the 'Gorblimey' can be seen being worn up to 1918.

19

20

**20 Private, Training Reserve Battalion, 1917.** He wears the soft SD cap introduced in 1917. Men in the TR battalions were not allocated to a particular regiment until posted, thus TR battalions did not wear cap badges; a tunic button backed with a circle of red cloth was worn instead. Training Reserve battalions were issued with cloth slip-on shoulder titles bearing the stitched or printed letters 'TR' in white on a khaki background. All NCOs and men wore the number of their TR brigade on their sleeve in the form of a cloth patch, the senior battalion in white, the others in descending order wore red, yellow, green, brown and blue. From May 1917 TR units became Graduated and Young Soldier Battalions and were once again aligned with specific regiments. The TR shoulder titles were discontinued from June 1917 and the sleeve number was also axed in December the same year.

21

**21 Battery Sergeant, Royal Field Artillery, c1916.** Where most line infantry wear their county shoulder titles in semi-circles, the Guards and Corps tended to display their titles in abbreviated form and in large bold letters. This Battery Sergeant clearly displays the letters 'RFA' on his shoulder and wears the white lanyard of the Artillery. He has recently suffered a close bereavement; soldiers were not permitted to wear black armbands for family mourning thus the second button on his tunic is covered in black cloth to denote mourning.

**22 Trooper, 1st Life Guards, c1915.** He has removed the stiffener from his cap and affects a style in the wear of the hat and the leather chin-strap often seen on soldiers who have returned from the front. As ever, the bandolier and breeches mark him as a member of a mounted unit; a top of a pair of leather gaiters can also just be observed. His cap badge, and shoulder titles of the numeral '1' and block letters 'LG', clearly delineate him to be serving with the 1st Life Guards.

**23 Roughrider Sergeant, Derbyshire Yeomanry, early 1915.** He wears the mounted troops' bandolier and Imperial Service badge denoting him a volunteer for overseas service. Above his stripes, a spur denotes him as a qualified Roughrider Sergeant.

23

24

**24 Farrier Sergeant, Derbyshire Yeomanry, 1915.** He is photographed mounted in his military saddle, rifle in holder by his side and sword drawn. Above his stripes is a horseshoe that denotes him as a qualified Farrier Sergeant. Troopers and soldiers with this same qualification wore the badge mid-way between their elbow and shoulder on the right arm of their tunic.

**25 Royal Artillery Wheeler, Wheelwright or Carpenter, c1915.** His trade is delineated by the wheel trade badge on his right sleeve. This example is a cloth badge but it was also widely common in brass.

25

**26 Armourer, Army Ordnance Corps, c1915.** His qualification badge for Armourer is a hammer and pincers worn on his right arm; the cap badge is that of the Army Ordnance Corps. He is wearing an economy jacket, made with no rifle patches or pleats in his pockets in late 1914/15 when stocks of material were short. Supplies also came piecemeal from different contractors and thus his trousers are clearly a different shade of khaki to his jacket.

26

27

**27 Lance Corporal Ernest Cole, Machine Gun Corps, c1917.** He proudly wears his machine gunner 'MG' qualification badge above his lance corporal stripe (these were also worn by MG-qualified soldiers in line infantry units). The Machine Gun Corps was created in 1915 and wore the MGC brass shoulder titles, but as seen here our soldier also wears cloth shoulder titles widely introduced from 1916.

28

**28 A Military Family, c1915.** Our private soldier is probably from one of the Service battalions of the Essex Regiment (his lack of puttees or belt suggest he may have been recalled from the Reserve). He has certainly seen previous military service as evinced by his good conduct stripes and his medal ribbons for the Queen's and King's South Africa medals. The ribbons are mounted on a brooch bar rather than sewn onto his tunic; this also could be an indication he has served in hot climes where detachable ribbons proved very useful due to the amount of regular washing required. Just above his left cuff are three Good-Conduct stripes.

29

**29 Corporal, 6th (Cyclist) Battalion, The Norfolk Regiment, 1914 (TF).** His cap badge and shoulder titles show his regiment and battalion, surmounted by the 'T', which shows he is a member of a Territorial Force Battalion. A little regimental research reveals the 6th Battalion of the Norfolk Regiment were a Territorial Cyclist Battalion. On his right breast he proudly wears an Imperial Service badge.

**30 Private Robert Hinton, 14th (Pioneer) Battalion, The Worcestershire Regiment, 1915-16.** The pick and shovel collar badge shows him to be a member of a pioneer battalion and in the case of the Worcestershire Regiment it reveals a fascinating story. The men of the line infantry pioneer battalions were not intended to be simply labour battalions but, inspired by Indian Army units, they were created as fully equipped battalions, skilled in constructive work but equally capable of fighting in the forefront of battle. This battalion were drawn from the Severn Valley by Colonel Sir Henry Webb, who raised it at his own expense. Originally known as the 'Severn Valley Pioneers', they were later designated the 14th (Pioneer) Battalion of the Worcestershire Regiment.

*30*

*31*

**31 Private, 10th (Service) Battalion, Royal Fusiliers, c1917.** He is wearing cloth division and battle insignia that point to the latter years of the war. He wears the collar badge of the battalion, a number '10' worn only upon the right-hand side of the collar – a unique distinction in the British Army. (The designation was unique to this battalion in the British Army but the first uniforms of the Canadian Expeditionary Force also had numbers on their collars, some surmounted with a 'C' but some not.) Often referred to as 'The Stockbroker's Battalion', it was originally raised in 1914 as one of the very first 'Pals Battalions'.

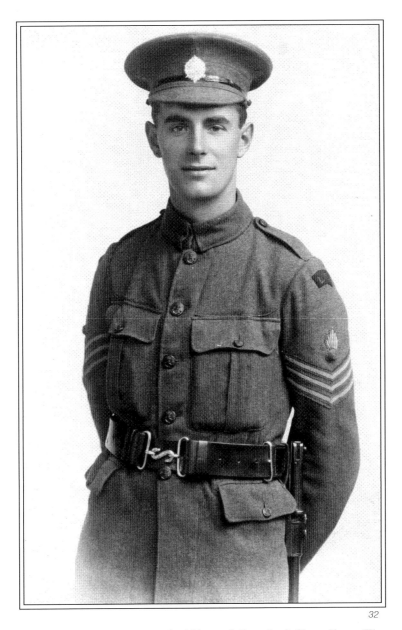

32

**32 Sergeant Bomber, 5th (City of London) Battalion, The London Regiment (London Rifle Brigade), c1916.** He is wearing LRB cloth shoulder titles and his bomber's badge worn above his stripes (he would lead bombing parties armed with Mills grenades to flush out the enemy from their dugouts and emplacements). Also note his regimental black 'horn' buttons.

33

**33 Royal Engineers, 1918.** A fine group, they are all wearing the blue and white armbands (the white was worn uppermost) which denote them as signallers or charged with signals responsibilities such as message-carrying by motorcycle. The Royal Corps of Signals was formed as a separate entity to carry out such duties in 1920.

**34 Sergeant, Royal Berkshire Regiment, 1915-16.** This smart NCO wears an economy tunic and Slade Wallace belt, with a Lee Metford or Long Lee bayonet. Unusually for an NCO, he is wearing what appear to be brown leather gloves and has a handkerchief peeping out from his cuff; with a smart cane in his hand too he may well be a 'Gentleman Ranker' (one who through breeding or education would have been able to take a Commission but chose to join the ranks). The rectangular patch of cloth in the regimental facing colour above his stripes was worn by NCOs and men of the 18th Division and means he was a member of 6th (Service) Battalion, Royal Berkshire Regiment and almost certainly one who was present with the battalion on the First Day of the Somme – 1 July 1916.

*34*

35

**35 Private, The Norfolk Regiment, c1916.** Wearing the 1908 Pattern webbing with ammunition pouch strap modification, he is holding a SMLE rifle with bayonet fixed. Note his puttees are worn in the figure of eight fashion rather than the usual spiral wind.

36

**36 Lance Corporal A. Armes, The Norfolk Regiment c1914.** He is smartly turned out wearing the 1914 Pattern equipment. The brown leather equipment was made from buffalo hide as a substitute for the 1908 webbing during the shortages of 1914/early 1915 but many soldiers went into combat with this same webbing. He holds a 'Long Lee' rifle with fixed bayonet, often used by Territorial and Service battalions especially when in training or on home service.

37

**37 Private, Motor Machine Gun Service, 1915.** Approval for the addition of a motor machine-gun battery to each Division was sanctioned in February 1915. These units were designated part of the Royal Field Artillery and were collectively known as the *Motor Machine Gun Service*. With its recruiting office in the Coventry offices of *Motor Cycle* magazine, men for the ranks of the MMGS were found from volunteers or by special enlistment of those known to be actively interested in motorcycles. These men mostly served on motorcycles with specially converted side-cars to take a machine gun and machine gunner. He wears the 1903 belt in 'pistol order' with separate haversack and water bottle – the standard rig for those early members of the MMGS.

*38*

*39*

**38 Tyneside Irish in Kitchener's Army, 1914.** No uniforms or badges were immediately available for these men so a strip of ribbon worn around their left arm was all they had to show they had enlisted. Officially numbered the 103rd (Tyneside Irish) Brigade, it contained four 'pals' battalions of volunteers from Newcastle-upon-Tyne. The brigade's four battalions were numbered 1st to 4th Tyneside Irish, when taken over by the British Army these becoming the 24th, 25th, 26th and 27th Battalions of the Northumberland Fusiliers. The trained battalions landed in France in January 1916 and first saw action in the Battle of the Somme.

**39 Two members of 8th Service Battalion, The Norfolk Regiment, 1914.** When in the early stages of training many of Kitchener's volunteers were not kitted out with uniform or equipment. Here two members of the 8th (Service) Battalion, sometimes referred to as the Norwich Businessman's Battalion, proudly wear their cap badges, their only item of uniform, in their lapels. Some of the men chosen as NCOs ended up tacking their stripes to their civvy jackets.

*40*

**40 Three new recruits.** The armbands (made from khaki material with a red crown) worn by these three recruits show they had joined under the Derby Scheme, 1915.

**41 Members of a Northamptonshire Regiment Service Battalion, c1914.** 'Kitchener Blues' had been introduced in an act of desperation when there was a chronic shortage of khaki uniforms in 1914/15.

**42 A 'Half and Half', 1915.** This soldier in a Norfolk Regiment service battalion wears the khaki service dress cap and puttees with his Kitchener Blue jacket and trousers.

*43*

**43 Field Kitchen, 2nd/5th Essex Regiment, c1915.** Catering for a battalion of 800-900 men at Milton Park, Peterborough, a number of the soldiers are wearing white working fatigues.

**44 Corporal, 2nd Battalion, West Yorkshire Regiment, 1914.** In 1914 most Regular Army Battalions of line infantry regiments were still on rotation whereby one battalion was on home service while the other was helping to garrison the Empire or serving on campaign. The smart khaki uniforms with long trousers with and without puttees, and insignia worn upon the pugaree of the Wolsey helmet, typify the look of the Regular soldier on foreign service in hot climes in 1914.

*44*

45

**45 Private, The Argyll & Sutherland Highlanders, 1914-15.** He wears the Glengarry with the regiment's unique dicing, and has a war economy jacket, but note it is the cut-away version issued to Scottish troops. He wears a 1914 Pattern leather belt, kilt and sporran, hose tops, spats and Highland shoes.

*46*

**46 Private, King's Own Scottish Borderers, c1914-15.** He is wearing another popular version of head dress worn by Scottish troops – the tam o'shanter.

47

**47 Private, 9th (Glasgow Highland) Battalion, The Highland Light Infantry, 1916.** Home on leave with his lassie, he is wearing a Balmoral bonnet, first pattern cutaway jacket, kilt, socks, short puttees and boots. This battalion was one of the first Territorial units to land in France in 1914 and fought at Festubert, Neuve-Chapelle and Loos in 1915, the Somme in 1916, Arras and Ypres in 1917, and went on to the bitter end, opposing the German spring offensive of spring 1918.

*48*

**48 Private, Black Watch (Royal Highlanders), 1916.** The Norwich photographer indicates this young soldier is probably 2nd/4th (City of Dundee) Battalion TF or 2nd/7th (Fife) Battalion TF, who were stationed in the city in 1916. He wears the distinctive midnight blue Glengarry and regimental cap badge and a standard army issue jacket with no cut-away (issued to Scottish troops when the cut-aways were in short supply), tall socks, puttees and dubbined boots.

49

**49 Lance Corporals, Highland Light Infantry, c1917.**
The Kirkcaldy photographer of this group, and the fact that they
are all well turned out young NCOs, suggests they were members
of the 53rd (Young Soldier) Battalion, HLI, a basic recruit training
unit based at Kirkcaldy, part of the Lowland Reserve Brigade that
was affiliated to the HLI in October 1917.

**50 Two Privates 2nd Battalion, The King's Own Yorkshire Light Infantry, 1914.** The bitterly cold winter of 1914/15 and the impracticalities of the long greatcoats issued to soldiers in the mud of the Western Front led to the first unofficial issue of goat and sheep skin jerkins in 1914. Practical and warm, the fleecy jerkins were nicknamed 'stinkers' because of the smell of the goatskin. They were officially replaced by a fur or blanket lined leather jerkin in 1916.

*50*

**51 Driver, Army Service Corps, c1915.** Taken 'at the front'. His ASC shoulder titles reveal his unit. His breeches, 1903 leather belt and private (or unit-purchased) boots and private purchase wristwatch suggest he was probably not a regular soldier but a Kitchener volunteer in 1914 and may have proceeded to France in 1915 with the first major divisions of the 'New Army'.

**52 Two Colour Sergeants and a Sergeant Major (centre), Gordon Highlanders, 'Somewhere in France', spring 1916.** The regiment of these soldiers may be discerned from their kilts, the colour sergeant on the right having removed his kilt apron to show the regimental tartan. The PH (Phenate-Hexamine) hood respirators in their bags (replaced by small box respirators between April and June 1916) are worn in place of their sporrans and they wear shrapnel helmets, first issued in late 1915.

*51*

*52*

*53*

**53 Stretcher Bearers, 2nd Battalion King's Shropshire Light Infantry, Salonika, 1916.** Stretcher bearing was always hot work, these soldiers are in shirt sleeve order and wear the distinctive 'SB' armbands of regimental stretcher bearers; also note their dog tags around their necks. Shorts were only issued in the later years of the First World War, thus in hotter climes until 1916 the majority of soldiers would wear long khaki drill (KD) trousers and puttees, but as the knees got torn out in action, for coolness and practicality soldiers cut down their trousers to make long shorts as seen here.

54

**54 Corporal, Canadian Expeditionary Force, France, 1916.** Identified as CEF by the 'General List' maple leaf and 'Canada' scroll collar badges, his tin helmet and PH gas mask date him to spring 1916, while his bandolier and CEF list collar badges suggest he was serving in a Corps. This picture is particularly rare for a family photo postcard – private photographers seldom got close enough to the front line troops to photograph them while they were caked in mud let alone when the mud was also still wet, as seen here.

**55 Private and Acting Lance Corporal, Cameron Highlanders, 1916.** Behind the lines, note the photographer has not even got a rug to put on the floor but some vain attempt at a backdrop has been rather poorly pinned up behind his subjects. One of them (standing) is an acting lance corporal, he wears his stripe on only one arm to denote this. Both have muddy boots and like all soldiers on active service they are making use of every available pocket for essential kit. I suspect the A/L.Cpl. has got his PH hood gas mask worn inside the jacket under his left hand and he maintains a shell dressing in his right pocket. Bulging upper pockets of both men may well contain soldiers' bibles or testaments, muster roll book (NCO only), cigarette packet, tin or case or lighter, army pay book and/or army 'small book', perhaps some keepsake letters and photographs, a watch and wallet.

55

**56 Junior NCOs Training Course, 1917.** Never assume a group photograph shows just one regiment, there are so many reasons for a military group photo. This one can be deduced from the fact the men are all well turned out, and caps have stiffener wires intact (one man, second from right on front row, wears the all-cloth 1917 pattern SD cap). Lack of mud or war-weary uniforms, and that they appear to be sitting in front of a purpose-built brick barracks, suggest this picture is taken at home and by the mixture of county regiments displayed on the cap badges that they have been brought together for a training course. They are all lance corporals with the exception of the sergeant in the centre. The standard purpose of the course for such an appointment would be to train the men in how to instruct both drill and musketry.

56

57

**57 Musketry Course, c1917.** The Sergeant Instructor seated centre wears the badge of the School of Musketry. The corporal wearing the badge of the Gloucestershire Regiment on the far left wears the medal ribbon of the Military Medal for Bravery in the Field (instituted in 1916). The rifles held by the group are P.14s and were commonly used by Second Line or Reserve troops.

58

**58 Signallers, Lincolnshire Regiment, c1918.** The heliographs, signal lamps and flags in front of this group, along with the crossed flags signaller qualifications worn by many, combined with the fact they all wear the same cap badge and shoulder titles without 'T' and battalion number above, indicate these are the signallers of a Regular or Service battalion of the Lincolnshire Regiment. A good indicator to date is that some wear overseas service chevrons first issued in 1918 (but backdated to 1914), some also have wounds stripes.

59

**59 14 Platoon D Company, 8th (Service) Battalion, The Lincolnshire Regiment, 1918.** The golden horseshoe Divisional patch, circle and bar beneath show them to be part of the 63rd Brigade (horseshoe), 37 Brigade (circle), while the bar beneath denoted the battalion. Some wear the overseas service stripes and date this picture accurately to 1918.

60

**60 Officers of a Royal Artillery Battery, 1918.** Probably one last gathering 'for the record' before demobilization, these officers show the mix of uniforms, different coloured breeches, cuff rank or rank pips on shoulder uniform worn at the end of the war. The cap badge of the field gun and the grenades on the collars all denote Royal Artillery (there is one exception, the Lieutenant in the middle of the back row is a member of the Army Service Corps). It did seem to hold true in this and many units, especially Corps, that the more senior officers had the tall leather boots and the junior officers had boots and puttees.

**61 Myths and Legends, 1915.** It was believed, particularly on the Western Front, that a bible carried in the breast pocket could stop a bullet. Many simply dismiss this as a myth but here is some proof with the bible carried by Private Hacket of the 1st Battalion, The Worcestershire Regiment – the bullet stopped on the last page.

THIS TESTAMENT SAVED THE LIFE OF P<sup>te</sup> W. HACKET 1<sup>st</sup> WOR REG<sup>t</sup> AT ARMENTIERES. AUG·20-1915–NOW IN 2<sup>ND</sup> GEN EASTERN HOSPITAL DYKE R<sup>D</sup> BRIGHTON · BULLET PASSING THROUGH OUTER COVER AND ALL THE LEAVES AND STOPPED AT THE LAST PAGE.

G·A·WILES          BRIGHTON

62

**62 Private, The Norfolk Regiment, 1914.**
This picture illustrates the issue greatcoat of 1914 with turn-back cuffs, rifle patches on the shoulders, single-breasted front and watch pocket. Soon, due to demand for new uniforms being such that material was at a premium, the greatcoat was produced without those extras.

**63 Private, Army Veterinary Corps, 1917.**
By 1915/16 officers were widely privately purchasing 'warms', a short double-breasted coat, and the short greatcoat or 'Cavalry Pattern' greatcoat for ORs followed soon after. Note our man's boots and spurs for mounted and driving duties and the waterproof cover on his cap.

63

**64 Private, Durham Light Infantry, October 1918.** The original image is nicely dated, and the all-cloth SD cap also helps confirm the late war (1917-18) period. His shoulder title shows the DLI bugle and county designation clearly and that he is not a Territorial, thus he served with either the Regular or Service battalions of the regiment.

**65 Corporal, East Lancashire Regiment, 1918.** A very fine study, he wears a full set of overseas service stripes for 1914-1918. Note the darker stripe nearest the cuff, this would have been in red and represented overseas service in 1914; all overseas service stripes for later years were in blue.

**66 Royal Artillery Bombardier, 1916.** His buttons show the field gun and crown of the Royal Artillery, on his arm can be seen the 'L' surrounded by the laurel of the Royal Artillery Gun Layer qualification badge. Most significant is the medal upon his left breast; the ribbon shows it to be the Military Medal for Bravery in the Field. When photographs show medals with extra long or unmounted ribbons on uniformed soldiers, this normally suggests the award has been made very recently and the recipient had gone to the photographic studio shortly after the presentation.

66

67

**67 Colour Sergeant (Acting CSM) Harry Daniels VC, 1915.** He is wearing his Victoria Cross awarded for gallantry at Neuve Chappelle, 1915. He is also wearing a waterproof cap cover and the black buttons (bugle and crown), chevrons and crown so distinctive of the Rifle Brigade. The VC remains our nation's highest award for gallantry 'in the face of the enemy'. Since its inception by Queen Victoria in 1856, fewer than 1,400 have been awarded.

68

**68 Prisoner of War, c1917.** A Private in the Manchester Regiment, he wears the dark uniform, polished peaked cap and armband of a prisoner of war in German hands. On his left breast is the number of his prison camp and personal prisoner number.

69

**69 Prisoner of War, c1917.** Another example of a British soldier in German captivity, in this case, a corporal of the Gordon Highlanders, who is not permitted his Glengarry or Tam but has to wear the standard peaked cap issued in German prison camp. Note his stripes worn on his right arm and his prisoner details worn on an armband upon the left.

70

**70 Allied Prisoners of War, c1917.** British servicemen are distinguishable in this mixed group by their dark uniforms but in this case a number of them have been allowed to keep their SD caps and regimental or corps cap badges. Look closely and you will spot their medal ribbons, good conduct and rank chevrons too.

**71 Private, The Suffolk Regiment, c1916.** He retains a khaki SD cap but the rest of his clothes are 'hospital blues', consisting of blue jacket and trousers, a white shirt and a scarlet tie. This soldier has been wounded or has suffered illness to the degree that he has 'caught a blighty' and been evacuated back to Britain (probably Abergavenny, Wales where this photo was taken), where he would have been in a military or auxiliary war hospital undergoing further treatment or convalescence.

71

**72 Lance Corporal, Army Service Corps (left) and Private, The Manchester Regiment, 1917.** Undoubtedly pals, both are wearing hospital blues under khaki greatcoats. Convalescent soldiers would be expected to wear their blue armbands on their greatcoats; if they took them off they could face a charge as it was thought they had done so for devious reasons such as going to a local pub, a dangerous deception if the man was on medication. Officers did not have hospital blues, they were trusted to wear just the armband.

**73 Private, The Leicestershire Regiment, c1919.** A real character, he wears the ribbon of the 1914 'Mons' Star and the insignia upon his arm shows he has qualified as a marksman. He has two good conduct stripes, and his wound stripes indicate that he was wounded on four separate occasions. I bet he had a tale to tell!

74

**74 Silver War Badge, c1917.** An ex-serviceman wearing his honourable discharge badge, instituted to signify he had 'done his bit' and to prevent accusations of evading military service.

75

**75 A Family Wedding, 1918.** So many of the men in this picture had 'done their bit'. The old soldier to the right of the bride serves with the Bedfordshire Regiment and has three good conduct stripes. The soldier immediately behind the groom serves in 9th Battalion, The Norfolk Regiment; he wears the ribbon of the 1914-15 Star. His four overseas service stripes, and the fact that the groom is still Royal Flying Corps, date the picture squarely to 1918. Note the 'O' and wing (brevet) on the groom's left breast which denotes he is a qualified Observer.

**76 Boy 1st Class, RN, 1914.** Although Royal Navy uniforms can look similar, the cap tally may reveal the most remarkable stories. This photograph shows Reginald Overton of Norwich, who was serving as a Boy 1st Class aboard HMS *Bulwark*. According to the Commonwealth War Graves Commission, he died on 26 November 1914: on that day HMS *Bulwark* accidentally blew up while she was moored in the estuary of the River Medway. All officers were killed by the explosion and only 14 sailors survived out of her complement of 750.

77

76

**77 Able Seamen, RN, 1914.** One of them, standing, is serving aboard HMS *Majestic*. The seated sailor is a member of the Royal Naval Reserve (as stated on his cap tally, 'RNR' is also marked on his right sleeve); both are wearing frocks, square rigs and sea jerseys. The photographer was based in Plymouth, this suggests the photograph was taken shortly after they joined HMS *Majestic*, which was one of the ships to escort the BEF to France in 1914. In November she transferred to the Humber and in December she became part of the Dover Patrol, further evidence to suggest the photograph would have been taken in August 1914.

*78*

**78 Royal Navy Rating, HMS *P.50*.** Sadly no arm badges can be seen so his branch or whether he was an Ordinary or a Leading Seaman cannot be discerned but, yet again, the cap tally reveals he served aboard the *P.50*, a patrol boat built under the Emergency War Programme. Patrol boats were built of mild steel for ramming submarines. Crewed by 50-54 men, these ships all served with the Dover patrol, Nore Local Defence Flotilla or Portsmouth escort force and worked ceaselessly to remove enemy mines from the channel. As you can imagine, this young man served in very dangerous waters.

*79*

**79 Stoker 2nd Class, RN, c1917.** He wears the white summer top on his cap and he is smartly turned out with horizontal concertina creases in his trousers. Sailors would try to effect seven or five such creases depending on the length of their legs. One old tale suggested these represented the seven seas or the five oceans. On his lower left arm he wears the badge of the Royal Navy Mines Clearance Service; the photograph dates to the later years of the war when cap tallies simply read 'HMS'.

**80 Royal Marine Light Infantry.** This photograph is annotated 1912 but it could have been taken anytime from when 'Broderick' caps were introduced for the RMLI in 1900, until after they served in the defence of Antwerp in 1914, although the earlier caps do appear to be slightly shallower and have wider crowns. They were very much like the caps of their comrades in the Royal Navy and the RMLI truly looked like 'soldiers of the sea'. After the Gallipoli campaign in 1915 the men of the RMLI adopted the standard SD caps when they were serving in the Battalions of the Royal Naval Division on the Western Front.

80

81

**81 Sub-Lieutenant, RN, c1915.** Officers' uniforms tended to have a slightly higher cut open collar than those found in the Second World War; rounded and winged detachable white collars, as well as narrow crowns and small peaks on caps are also good indicators of an early 20th century vintage. This photograph is annotated '2nd in Command HM Submarine *E.21*' – a submarine commissioned in October 1915.

82

**82    Lieutenant    Commander,    RN,  annotated October 1916.** Wearing a white cap cover in October shows the officer depicted was on service in a hot climate, such as the Mediterranean. The braid on this officer's cuff is not sewn directly onto the material of his sleeve, instead a distinction cloth backing appears behind them.

*83*

**83 Ordinary Telegraphist, Royal Naval Volunteer Reserve, c1914.** His trade badge consisting of wings and lightning bolt may be seen on his upper right arm. Note the three wavy bands on his square rig, a theme carried on in the cuff lace of RNVR officers and giving the force the nickname of the 'wavy navy'.

**84 Flight Lieutenant Observer, Royal Naval Air Service, c1915.** Note that rather than a naval anchor in the centre of his cap badge there is an eagle, and winged 'O's are displayed above the rank lace upon his cuff delineating him an Observer.

*84*

85

**85 Air Mechanic, Royal Naval Air Service, Winter 1916.** Their uniforms do look like those worn by ratings and officers in the Royal Navy, but look closer for spread eagles on their insignia, as worn by this rating on his right arm.

**86 Sergeant Observer, Royal Naval Air Service (RAF), 1918.** He wears a khaki uniform with a khaki integral belt introduced in 1918, his buttons have a circlet of rope with the crown and eagle of the RNAS in the centre. His cap cover would be of khaki material and his winged 'O' brevet denotes he is a qualified Observer. Although he does not wear them (the picture was taken during the RNAS and RFC changeover to RAF), such tunics as these would be the first to carry the RAF eagle on each shoulder.

86

**87 Second Lieutenant, Royal Flying Corps, 1916.** He wears the distinctive side hat, 'maternity' jacket and breeches of officers commissioned directly into the RFC, along with bronze cap and collar badges with the letters 'RFC' surrounded in a wreath surmounted by a King's crown. On his left breast he wears the wings of a RFC pilot. The rank insignia were displayed in the form of cloth or metal pips on the epaulettes.

87

88

**88 Second Lieutenant, Royal Flying Corps, 1918.** Another version of the RFC officer's uniform is seen here with the standard serge officer's tunic, RFC wings and brass RFC buttons. This style of uniform was also adopted by officers who volunteered for the RFC from regiments or corps but such transfer officers usually retained the collar badges of their parent regiment or corps.

**89 Trainee Pilot, Royal Air Force, 1918.** The trainee status of this young man with his mother is denoted by the white band around his hat. He is one of the first to wear an RAF Blue uniform.

89

90

**90 Lieutenant, Royal Air Force, 1918.** In the early months of the newly created RAF in 1918, a new system of rank insignia was adopted. Note the early officers' caps had shiny peaks and bars either side of the cap badge. These bars indicate a Second Lieutenant or a Lieutenant.

91

**91 Air Mechanic Second Class, Royal Flying Corps, c1916.** A smartly turned out chap with a fine moustache and swagger cane for walking out, he has probably volunteered from a Regular Army unit for the RFC. He wears the typical RFC other ranks' uniform of worsted 'maternity' jacket and breeches and undoubtedly would be wearing tall puttees and boots. Unlike the officers he does not wear the Sam Browne leather belt, but he does have the cloth shoulder title 'Royal Flying Corps'.

**92 Air Mechanic, Royal Air Force, c1919.** One of the first to wear the brand new RAF badge. That is, however, the only change as our man retains his old RNAS cap with braided cap band, khaki jacket and RNAS buttons. He does not appear to have the cloth eagles on his shoulders.

*92*

**93 Volunteer Training Corps, 1914.** Before they were issued uniforms, several VTC units struck their own lapel badges and were assigned training sergeants from the Army Reserve, as seen on the left of this photo.

*93*

**94 & 95 Volunteer Training Corps Officer (left) and Volunteer (right), 1915.** Our officer clearly has previous military experience, he is wearing a Queen's South Africa medal with five bars awarded for service during the Anglo-Boer war (1899-1902). He wears no cap badge; many units got their full uniforms before they had designed their own badge. Although a similar colour to the officer's uniform, the cut for Volunteers was not as good; they wore gaiters, puttees or no protection on their lower legs and would wear their own boots. Volunteers (the name for other ranks in the VTC) also wore red armbands with large black 'GR' (Georgius Rex – King George V) letters.

94

95

**96 City of Cambridge Volunteers (VTC).**
Two members pose for the camera. Both wear
the VTC Association badge in the buttonhole
of their top right pockets and their VTC badge
on their hats. The standing volunteer wears
his VTC marksman's proficiency badge on the
right forearm of his tunic.

**97 Lincolnshire Volunteers (VTC), 1918.**
Members of the shooting team, armed with
P.14 rifles. The NCOs and privates all wear
General List badges, whereas the officer wears
the badge of the county regiment.

96

97

**98 Scottish Volunteer Training Corps, 1918.** They wear black balmoral bonnets with red dicing and General Service badges. Their uniforms are standard khaki with 1914 Pattern belt and pouches with no cross straps. They are carrying their P.14 rifles at the slope.

*98*

**99 Lieutenant of the Volunteers after the July 1918 reforms.** He wears the same style of uniform and has a cuff rank tunic similar to a Regular or Territorial Army officer, but his buttons and badges show the lion and unicorn of the General List and he wears a letter 'V' for Volunteers on his collar.

*99*

**100 North Walsham Platoon of the Volunteers, 1918.** Nicknamed the 'Walsham Old and Bold'. Unlike many of their counterparts, a number of their county regiment cap badges (The Norfolk Regiment) were obtained for both the officers and men of this unit.

*100*

**101 Australian Imperial Force Officer and his Bride, England, 1916.** After defeat at Gallipoli the ANZAC forces underwent a major reorganisation. Significant for our photograph, the Australian 3rd Division was sent directly to England in preparation for their crossing to France and entry onto the Western Front. Many romances blossomed in the short time the colourful Aussie soldiers were in Britain.

**102 Private, Australian Imperial Force, 1916.** There can be a problem with identification because the AIF did not employ regimental badges but (with only one exception) wore the standard AIF badge in cap and on collar. If an OR's shoulder strap or officer's collar can be observed, an indication to unit may be discerned.

*102*

*103*

**103 Vesta Tilley in the Uniform of a Private, Royal Engineers, 1915.** Tilley's popularity as a music hall male impersonator reached its all-time high point during the First World War when she and her husband ran a military recruitment drive, in the guise of characters like 'Tommy in the Trench' and 'Jack Tar Home from the Sea'. Many wives and girlfriends followed her lead by being photographed in their partner's uniform but it was considered rather daring.

**104 Navy and Army Canteen Board, 1918.**
A uniformed employee; although her cap badge
is obscured, her woven shoulder title states
'NACB', forerunner of the NAAFI.

*104*

*105*

**105 Women's Legion, c1917.** The women's
units attached to the British Army in 1916/17
all wore similar uniforms with four-pocket tunics
usually with integral belts (First Aid Nursing
Yeomanry, FANY, units were the notable
exception – all ranks wore a Sam Browne belt),
long skirts and a wide-brimmed brown felt hat.
On it is worn the badge consisting of a laurel
wreath surmounted by the letters 'WL' with
a robed female figure of 'Victory' with raised
laurels in hand.

106

**106 Officer, Women's Forage Corps, c1916.** Despite often wearing polished brass badges, female officers can be discerned by the pockets in the skirt of their jacket. From 1917 the officers tended to wear bronze cap and collar badges similar to the ASC star and laurel but with no crown and 'FC' in scrolled letters in the centre. She also wears a peaked cap with a storm flap at the rear, preferred by the drivers of motor vehicles.

107

**107 Workers, Women's Auxiliary Army Corps, 1917.** Note their woven shoulder titles and cap badges in brass; officers wore bronze. The first WAACs proceeded to France in March 1917; by 1918, 6,000 were serving there.

**108 Women's Auxiliary Army Corps Worker c1917.** The photograph shows the standard overall-type uniform worn by WAACs, made in khaki gabardine.

108

109

**109 Workers, Queen Mary's Auxiliary Army Corps, 1918.** Note the 'QM' for 'Queen Mary's' armbands on their greatcoats. Be they WAACs or QMAACS, their roles did not change and they carried on with their often unglamorous tasks, such as maintaining lines of communication and working as cooks, clerks, telephonists and drivers.

110

**110 Technical Worker, Women's Royal Naval Service, 1918.** Created in 1917, the first uniformed WRNS appeared in 1918. Most Wrens were given a trade category denoted by blue non substantive trade badges viz:
Scallop shell - Household Worker
Three spoked wheel – Motor Driver
An arrow crossed by a lightning flash - Signals
Crossed keys – Storekeepers, Porters and Messengers
Crossed quill pens - Clerical Staff
Envelope - Postwomen and Telegraphists
Crossed hammers - Technical Worker
  By 1918 there were 5,500 Wrens. The WRNS was disbanded in 1919.

**111 Women's Forage Corps, 1918.** By 1918 many female officers had taken to wearing leather belts. Also note the Forewoman (three stripes) has an overall dress with an open collar worn with a collar and tie. Army stripes are worn on their gabardine dresses to denote female NCOs and some of the female drivers appear to have adopted entire male uniform for their duties; this was not unique but still an unusual thing to see in 1918. They look a motley crew but would

*111*

be working hard in chaffing stores and forage centres to supply the army's constant need for forage for their horses.

*112*

**112 Women's Royal Air Force, 1919.** The last of the women's services to be formed, the WRAF carried out very similar duties to the WAAC, especially supplying drivers and mechanics to 'free a man for the Front'. The WRAF was disbanded in 1920.

# The Inter-War Years
## 1919-1938

The years immediately after the First World War saw the British Army dust itself down and start to address its new role as a peacetime army. There was still, however, the occupation of the Rhineland, with many British troops based in and around Cologne – a postcard photograph of a British soldier embossed or printed with the name of a Cologne photographer is normally a good indicator that an ancestor was part of the army of occupation.

Following the Armistice the Territorial Force units were gradually stood down and disbanded. New recruiting started in early 1920 and the Territorial Force was reconstituted shortly afterwards. On 1 October 1920 the Territorial Force was renamed the Territorial Army. The 1st Line divisions (that were created in 1907 or 1908) were reconstituted in that year. However, the composition of the divisions was altered, with a reduction in the number of infantry battalions and units of cavalry. Of the 55 yeomanry regiments, only the 14 senior regiments retained their horses. The remaining yeomanry were converted to artillery or armoured car units, or disbanded.

Throughout the 1920s and 1930s the training structure was similar to the pre-First World War years in that the recruit was put through his paces in drill and rifle, but with the addition of new weaponry such as machine guns and up-to-date mortars. All potential recruits were advised upon joining that the TA provided a field force to supplement the Regular Army *either* in defence of this country *or* the defence of British interests abroad. No longer would a TA soldier be asked if he would volunteer for active service abroad, when you enlisted in the TA it was part of your obligation.

The Regular Army looked to its responsibilities across the Empire and garrisons in India were enlarged and reinforced, with a number of duties along the North West Frontier and Afghanistan; look out for the India General Service Medal and ribbon on the uniform of your ancestor. Indeed, tours as far away as China and America were undertaken by a number of line infantry units – it was once again true to say on the recruitment posters, 'Join the Army and See the World' (7).

In the years after the war a number of regiments were given the prefix 'Royal' as a mark of regal acknowledgement for their outstanding deeds in the Great War. Some regiments were also redesignated, such as the Bedfordshire Regiment (3).

During the inter-war years the muddy and war-tired image of the British Tommy was replaced by the bright smiling faces of new young Regular Army and Territorial soldiers in well pressed uniforms with smart, stiffened caps and shiny badges, boots and buttons (2, 3, 4). Indeed, more buttons and badges: the old general list lion and unicorn buttons of the First World War were replaced by regimentally marked buttons for other ranks, the sergeants began to wear their red sashes again and collar badges were issued to all ranks. Officers retained their cap and collar badges in bronze and wore jackets tailored with open necks for wear with collar and tie. NCOs and other ranks still wore high-neck service dress with collar badges in white metal or brass or a combination of both, depending on regimental preference.

Fatigues (2, 5, 6) would often be worn when the men were undergoing field training, especially when tackling obstacle courses, bayonet fighting and field engineering works, or rifle training, for instance, at Bisley. National shooting competitions and rifle training have been conducted there since the National Rifle Association was granted a Royal Charter in 1894 and continues to this day to promote 'marksmanship in the interests of the Defence of Realm and permanence of the Volunteer Forces, Navy, Military and Air'. The contest to find the Champion marksman in the Army, who would be awarded the prestigious Army Best Shot Medal, sometimes referred to as the 'King's (or Queen's) Medal', is still held annually at Bisley.

In the Royal Air Force, the major change in uniform was for other ranks, who finally were issued with the full blue worsted uniforms (8).

## Medal Detective

Far more group photographs of very smart and polished soldiers turn up from the 1920s and 1930s than in any other period, when troops are photographed in the likes of shooting teams and a massive array of sporting groups from running, cricket and hockey to football, boxing and rugby. Look out for soldiers, sailors and airmen who had served in the First World War and remained in or rejoined the Territorials or Regulars, who can normally be detected because of the medal ribbons they wear.

Those who had fought at Mons and in the opening battles of the war wear a 1914 Star (colloquially known as the 'Mons Star'), approved in 1917 for issue to officers and men of British forces who served in France or Belgium between 5 August and midnight 22/23 November 1914. The former date is the day after Britain's declaration of war against the Central Powers, and the closing date marks the end of the First Battle of Ypres. A bronze clasp on the medal ribbon, or a small silver rosette worn with just a bar of ribbons, denotes the recipient was under fire during the qualification period.

If the tri-colour ribbon is seen without rosette, it means either the recipient was not under fire in 1914 or, far more likely, that he is the recipient of the 1914-15 Star. The 1914-15 Star was approved in 1918, for issue to officers and men of British and Imperial forces who served in any Theatre of the War between 5 August 1914 and 31 December 1915 (other than those who had already qualified for the 1914 Star; no man *should* have been awarded both a Mons Star and a 1914-15 Star but there are some known anomalies). With the exception of members of the Royal Naval Division involved in the Defence of

Antwerp, most men of the Royal Navy, even if they were killed in 1914, were not awarded the 1914 Star.

With both the 1914 and 1914-15 Stars, a British War Medal and a Victory Medal would be worn. The British War Medal and Allied Victory Medal were both approved in 1919, for issue to officers and men of British and Imperial forces who had rendered service between 5 August 1914 and 11 November 1918. Officers and men of the Royal Navy, Royal Marines, and Dominion and Colonial naval forces (including reserves) were required to have completed 28 days' mobilised service. These medals were automatically awarded in the event of death on active service before the completion of this period. Both medals extended to cover the period 1919-20 and service in mine-clearing at sea, as well as participation in operations in North and South Russia, the eastern Baltic, Siberia, the Black Sea, and the Caspian Sea.

Most of the Territorials who had volunteered in 1914 went to war in 1915 and received the classic trio of First World War Medals: 1914-15 Star, British War Medal and Allied Victory Medal (nicknamed Pip, Squeak and Wilfred after newspaper cartoon characters). But for those who did not qualify for a Star and met the criteria of having been embodied before 30 September 1914 and had completed four years' service before that date, and to have served outside the UK between 4 August 1914 and 11 November 1918, there was the Territorial Force War Medal. Many of the recipients of these medals were members of the cyclist battalions who had remained on Home Defence duties until 1916. Because of the strict criteria of this medal it is without doubt the scarcest of all the standard British medals of the First World War – only 34,000 were awarded, compared, for example, with the 1914-15 Star, of which no fewer than 2,350,000 were awarded. Long Service in the Territorial Force was recognised with the award of the Territorial Force Efficiency Medal, granted for 12 years' efficient service (war service counted double). This medal was superseded in 1921 when the Territorial Force was renamed the Territorial Army.

*1*

**1 Territorial Battalion Band, The Leicestershire Regiment, c1925.** All band members are turned out in smart scarlet uniforms and a few of the officers and men wear trios and pairs of First World War medals. On 1 October 1920 the Territorial Force was renamed the Territorial Army.

2

**2 Two Lance Corporals and a Sergeant (far right), Royal Berkshire Regiment, c1925.** Inter-war year soldiers are made distinctive by the slightly different SD caps (note the wider peak). The old soft version SD cap can also be seen being worn on manoeuvres and for fatigues but the last of these were issued in the early 1930s and were truly obsolete by the time of the Second World War. Soldiers were certainly becoming smarter again.

3

**3 Regular Soldiers of The Bedfordshire & Hertfordshire Regiment, c1925.** No shortage of kit here and this turnout would please any sergeant major. The Bedfordshire Regiment was retitled and rebadged The Bedfordshire & Hertfordshire Regiment in July 1919 in recognition of the contribution of men from Hertfordshire during the Great War.

**4 Signal Section, The Essex Regiment, 1932.** Gone are the hats with wire removed. War service stripes had not been worn since 1920 but still the brass crossed flags of the qualified signallers remain. In general, uniforms could be standardised and the expectation of smartness had returned to the British army by the 1930s when the men spent more time on the parade ground than the battlefield.

4

5

5 **Northamptonshire Regiment, 1930s.** Soldiers of the regiment enjoying 'Happy Days at Bisley' in the 1930s. The men are in short sleeve order and are wearing their fatigues; I suspect they have finished their camp chores and are looking forward to a mess social. Bisley always has enjoyed a fine reputation with the British Army.

6

**6 Privates, The Norfolk Regiment c1934.** These soldiers are wearing their fatigues with full 1908 webbing and they hold SMLE rifles with fixed bayonets.

**7 Corporal, The Northamptonshire Regiment, c1930.** Our soldier, a veteran of the First World War (wearing his British War Medal and Victory Medal), is dressed in khaki drill (KD) uniform. Jacket and shorts with tall puttees and hose tops were everyday wear for military duties in hot climates such as India. Long trousers without puttees for walking out – still with a swagger cane of course! Badges on these uniforms are often only pinned on because they would require regular laundering. In garrisons such as India every soldier could afford a servant to wash and iron their uniforms and thus the standard of their turnout was very high.

7

8

**8 Aircraftsmen, RAF, 1924.** Newly passed out, at last they wear the full blue worsted uniforms complete with the eagles on the shoulders, with high collar, integral belt, breeches, tall blue puttees and black boots. Each man carried a swagger cane for walking out.

# The Second World War

## 1939-1945

From the late 1930s a far more utilitarian approach was directed towards British Army units. Service dress and 1908 Pattern equipment was phased out and replaced by the new 1937 Pattern web equipment and battledress. Although some units, especially Territorials, were still in the old service dress and 1908 webbing (or at least elements of it) in 1939 (1) – and indeed many men did proceed to France with the BEF wearing the same – for the majority, gone were the polished regimental buttons, stiff caps and tall puttees, all of them replaced by a khaki woollen battle dress jacket and trousers. The jacket was fastened up to the neck for NCOs and other ranks; the officers, as ever, wore theirs with open collar, shirt and tie. Breast pockets were pleated and trousers had a shell dressing pocket on the right just below the waist and a map pocket on the left leg. Unlike in the First World War, they were also issued shrapnel helmets and gas masks.

When war was declared in 1939 conscription was introduced immediately in the form of legislation known as the National Service (Armed Forces) Act, under which all men between 18 and 41 were made liable for conscription. By the end of 1939 over one and a half million men had been recruited into the armed forces. Of these, 1,128,000 joined the British Army and the remainder were equally divided between the Royal Navy and the Royal Air Force. The registration of all men in each age group in turn began on 21 October for those aged 20 to 23. By May 1940, registration had extended only as far as men aged 27 and did not reach those aged 40 until June 1941.

A useful tip for identifying soldiers in studio portraits during the early war years, when the winters were snowy and so cold the sea froze in places, is that there was a marked vogue at the time for wearing their greatcoats with collars turned up. This was against dress regulations so it was rather daring, as well as giving the subject a certain 'film star' quality (3, 35).

Soldiers between 1939 and 1941 are identified by a combination of 1937 Pattern uniform and webbing, stiff peaked caps, khaki side hats and a distinct lack of formation signs and insignia (6, 7, 9, 23). On the shoulders of battle dress uniforms, both brass and slip-on titles (worsted backing with black lettering) bearing the name of the regiment to which the soldier belonged, were standard. Below that on the upper arm, an arm of service stripe can be found from 1940. At this period in time just one stripe was worn on each upper arm in such colours as red for infantry, red and blue equal halves for Royal Artillery, blue and red equal halves for Royal Engineers, green for infantry rifle regiments and half yellow, half blue for Royal Army Service Corps.

Officers frequently wore peaked caps with bronze cap badges for their corps or infantry unit; their rank, rather than regimental titles, would be worn on their shoulders. Brass rank insignia are known but most officers chose the far more practical cloth insignia, again with coloured backing to denote infantry or corps units. Officers were issued different webbing to that of NCOs and ORs, which consisted of belt, cross straps, binocular case, revolver holster, ammunition pouch, compass case, map board, side pack and small pack, all of which was worn in a variety of styles, often to suit the duties of the officer when in the field. Indeed, many officers adopted the same webbing as the men when in combat for reasons of practicality and to reduce their chances of drawing fire by being recognised as an officer.

Officers' service dress worn for light duties and parades had changed little since the end of the First World War, but was seen less frequently as the war went on. However, long trousers and shoes (not breeches, tall puttees and boots as favoured into the 1920s and early 1930s) are the standard kit for officers' service dress during the Second World War (18, 19).

From 1940 all services were the subject of initially occasional, then standard issue economy battledress tunics. The 1940 Pattern tunic had no pleats in the pocket and no cover flaps for its buttons (apart from the fly zip of the battledress trousers).

After initial opposition in 1939, following Dunkirk the thinking about cloth formation signs on battledress changed and they were permitted in an effort to reinforce the group identity and *esprit de corps* of the rebuilt British Army. Formation signs are widely seen being worn by soldiers on home service from September 1940 (7). Arm of service stripes were soon also used in conjunction with Divisional insignia to denote brigade seniority. In 1943 slip-on shoulder titles were replaced by coloured, semi-circular printed cloth shoulder titles (woven versions of the same badge were usually only available in the early years as private-purchase or 'bazaar made' items) (8, 9). By the end of the war, with the introduction of service stripes and all this variety of insignia and trade qualification badges, and even coloured berets for some units, pre-war sergeant majors were to comment that the men looked like '******* Christmas trees!'

Although maroon, the beret of the British Parachute Regiment is often known as the 'red beret' and has become synonymous with elite airborne forces (16). This distinctive head-dress was officially introduced in 1942, at the direction of General Frederick Browning, commander of the British 1st Airborne Division. The colour of the beret was reportedly chosen by his wife, the novelist Daphne du Maurier, and was first worn in action by the men of the Parachute Regiment in North Africa during November 1942. Shaping berets is a comparatively modern affectation, during the Second World War berets were decidedly generous in proportion.

Khaki berets were adopted as early as 1942. With the introduction of the shapeless GS cap in September 1943, many more officers chose to wear the khaki beret with pride (20, 21, 22, 23).

The Royal Navy also adopted battledress for certain operational duties, especially around 1944, but it was never widely adopted for all officers and ratings. The cap tally could once again be the most informative clue in a photograph, but for reasons of security and ease of production tallies were reduced to simply read 'HMS' (26, 27, 28), which does not make the job of family historians any easier.

The RAF moved away from four-pocket service dress for officers and men from late 1940 when the first battledress jackets and trousers were introduced for air crew, fully adopted in 1941 and worn by all ranks and trades from 1943. As standard, there was no belt with this uniform, but if aircrew did decide to carry a sidearm, a belt and pistol would be worn (unless he chose to stuff the revolver down the side of his flying boot).

The Women's Services had proved themselves more than capable of 'doing their bit' in the First World War and, on the eve of the Second World War, all three arms of service had re-established female branches – the Auxiliary Territorial Service (ATS) in 1938, Women's Royal Naval Service (WRNS) and Women's Auxiliary Air Force (WAAF) in 1939. They remained all-volunteer units until December 1941 when unmarried women aged between 20 and 30 became liable for conscription under the National Service Act. Later, married women were made liable to be directed into war-related civilian work, although pregnant women and mothers with young children were completely exempt.

Created under a Royal Warrant in 1902, the Queen Alexandra's Imperial Military Nursing Service (QAIMNS) was named after the then queen, who became its President. From 30 May 1941 QAIMNS (40) personnel were granted emergency commissions and wore rank insignia corresponding to their equivalent Army rank: Sister (Lieutenant); Senior Sister (Captain); Matron (Major); Principal Matron (Lieutenant-Colonel); Chief Principal Matron (Colonel); Matron-in-Chief (Brigadier).

Up to 1941 ATS officers wore their own unique badges of rank on their shoulders. In 1941 they adopted the standard British Army pips, crown etc but retained their old titles. Their officer rank structure and equivalent army ranks were: Second Subaltern (Second Lieutenant); Subaltern (Lieutenant); Junior Commander (Captain); Senior Commander (Major); Chief Commander (Lieutenant-Colonel); Controller (Colonel); Senior Controller (Brigadier); Chief Controller (Major-General).

The WRNS (44) was raised again in 1939. By December of that year there were 3,000 Wrens and by 1944 the service had reached its peak membership of 74,620. Wrens were employed in a variety of jobs including plotters, bomb range markers, despatch riders, communications, meteorology, boat crews and even cinema operators. WRNS ranks and Royal Navy equivalents 1939-1945 were: Ordinary Wren (Ordinary Seaman); Wren (Able Seaman); Leading Wren (Leading Seaman); Petty Officer Wren (Petty Officer); Chief Wren (Chief Petty Officer); Third Officer (Sub Lieutenant); Second Officer (Lieutenant); First Officer (Lieutenant Commander); Chief Officer (Commander); Superintendent (Captain); Commandant (Commodore); Chief Commandant (Rear Admiral).

The WAAF (45) was created in June 1939, absorbing the 48 RAF companies of the Auxiliary Territorial Service. From February 1940 it was no longer possible to enter directly as an officer; all officers were appointed from the ranks. From July 1941 WAAF officers held full commissions. WAAFs were involved in such duties as parachute packing, manning of barrage balloons, catering, meteorology, radar, transport, telephonic and telegraphic duties. They also worked in top secret areas with codes, on intelligence operations and in reconnaissance photograph analysis. WAAFs were a vital presence in the control of aircraft, both at the radar stations and, iconically, as plotters in the operation rooms, most notably during the Battle of Britain.

The ranking system changed in part in 1941 (differently named pre-1941 ranks are given in italics): Aircraftwoman 2nd Class (Aircraftman 2nd Class); Aircraftwoman 1st Class (Aircraftman 1st Class); Leading Aircraftwoman (Leading Aircraftman); *Assistant Section Leader* Corporal (Corporal); *Section Leader* Sergeant (Sergeant); *Senior Section Leader* Flight Sergeant (Flight Sergeant); Under Officer (Warrant Officer); *Company Assistant* Assistant Section Officer (Pilot Officer); *Deputy Company Commander* Section Officer (Flying Officer); *Company Commander* Flight Officer (Flight Lieutenant); *Senior Commandant* Squadron Officer (Squadron Leader); *Chief Commandant* Wing Officer (Wing Commander); *Controller* Group Officer (Group Captain); *Senior Controller* Air Commandant (Air Commodore); Air Chief Commandant (Air Vice-Marshal).

After months in civvies with armbands and scant uniforms, in July 1940 Winston Churchill took a personal interest in the development and equipment of the Home Guard (46, 47, 48). In August 1940 units were officially affiliated to their county regiments and permission to wear the county regiment cap badges was granted; in February 1941 the War Office sanctioned full commissions to Home Guard officers. Their rank insignia was displayed on plain worsted backing and followed the standard ranks system of the British Army. See Appendix II for a list of Home Guard county designations.

As the war widened our service personnel served in hot climes and cold lands, so many family albums will no doubt have private snapshots of their relatives in a variety of uniforms – some in khaki drill from the desert, some in jungle green from India (11, 12) and Burma, while others are rugged up for patrols around the Atlantic and upon the Russian convoys. But remember these are rare, so don't be disappointed if there are only studio photographs of your relatives. Cameras were few and far between, film was difficult to obtain and often a camera could not be used due to security reasons.

However, there was the AFPU (Army Film and Photographic Unit). Many British official photographs are held by the Imperial War Museum and if you manage to track your ancestor's unit down I think it well worth arranging a visit – you never know who you might recognise on the photos, some are even named. Even if you don't find a picture specifically showing your ancestor, the trip need not be a waste of time, indeed far from it. If you manage to get photographs of their unit in action it will bring you closer to your ancestor by allowing you to see some of the things he or she saw and some of the people they served with.

How the British Soldier of 1939 Goes to War

STEEL HELMET
2½ lbs.

ANTI-GAS CAPE
3½ lbs.

RESPIRATOR
(in "ALERT" Position)
3½ lbs.

HAVERSACK
& CONTENTS
5 lbs.

STRAPS, BELT etc.
3½ lbs.

POUCHES
(Each containing
60 Rounds Bren
Gun ammunition)
10 lbs each.

BAYONET
& SCABBARD
1¾ lbs.

RIFLE
8 lbs 10½ ozs.

THE "battle dress" of the British Army was finally approved in April 1939, and is now worn by both men and officers. It is a two-piece garment of khaki serge, consisting of a blouse and trousers buckling at the wrists and ankles, the ankles also being protected by web anklets. The weight of the uniform is about 12 lb. This soldier is wearing battle dress, but is not completely equipped. When wearing full marching order, the infantryman carries a valise (or pack) on his back in place of the haversack seen here, the latter being transferred to the left hip above the bayonet and counter-balanced on the right by a water-bottle.
The valise holds the great-coat, cardigan when not worn, and such other personal effects as individual skill in packing can get into it; while in the haversack are a hold-all with comb, tooth-brush, shaving outfit, fitted housewife, socks, mess tin, emergency ration, etc. The large patch pocket on the trousers is to hold maps and papers. Though officers carry some additional articles of equipment, such as revolvers and binoculars and compasses, there is nothing in their uniform to distinguish them from the men except the shoulder badge.

ANKLE BOOTS
4¾ lbs.

Specially photographed for THE WAR ILLUSTRATED under War Office supervision

*1*

**1 'How the British Soldier Went to War in 1939.'** Most soldiers did indeed have this uniform and webbing set, introduced from 1937. But a number of battalions, particularly the so-called 'Militia' battalions and Territorials, so hastily expanded in the late 1930s, still had 1908 Pattern webbing. The greatcoats worn by soldiers were also of the single-breasted type and almost as long as those from the First World War; indeed some units, especially corps, did serve in France wearing service dress and many men carried SMLE rifles of First World War vintage.

2

**2 Gunner Ernest Griffin, Royal Artillery, 1940.** Here is the author's great-uncle, looking very smart in his service dress with SD cap and all-polished brass buttons and badges in 1940. The gun badge on the cap, with grenade collar badges, signifies he is Royal Artillery; the RA shoulder title confirms this nicely. In the First World War the RA white lanyard was worn over the left shoulder but in 1920 the lanyard was moved to the right shoulder because of the problem of trying to remove the knife on the end of the lanyard from the pocket underneath the bandolier. Even though the bandoliers were seldom worn by 1940, the white lanyard remained on the right.

3

**3 Private, The Royal Norfolk Regiment, 1940.** In 1940 it seemed to be quite the vogue to have your photograph taken in greatcoat (breaking the dress regulations which stated your collar should not be turned up) and SD cap. He wears a comforter at his neck and the collar and brass 'dish' buttons of his 1937 battledress blouse may be seen in the open collar of his greatcoat.

*4*

**4 Signalman, Royal Signals, 1940.** Smartly turned out, with polished regimental buttons, cap and collar badges; on his left arm he has the dark blue lanyard – worn on the service dress to signify the regiment's origins in the Royal Engineers.

*5*

**5 Corporal, Royal Norfolk Regiment, 1940.** Older men were called up for war service from the reserve during the Second World War. Our corporal wears the ribbons of his British War and Victory medals, awarded for service in the First World War. His service dress with regimental buttons worn with a side cap suggest a date of late 1940, when much kit had been lost at Dunkirk and many soldiers were kitted out with service dress from regimental stocks.

6

**6 Three pals just out of training, 1941.** The 1937 pattern battledress had distinctive pleated pockets and flaps of material to cover buttons. These men are in the 'walking out' order of uniform with no webbing, no gaiters, and shoes.

**7 Private, The Lincolnshire Regiment 1940/41.** The early period of this photo is suggested by the 1937 pattern battledress blouse with cloth slip-on shoulder titles (worn until 1943).

*7*

*8*

**8 Artificer Sergeant, Royal Electrical and Mechanical Engineers, 1943.** He is dressed in a 1940 Pattern battledress blouse and wears the arm of service stripe and printed shoulder titles but no formation badge above the distinctive hammer and tongs and three chevrons which denote an Artificer Sergeant (transferred to REME 1942). Shoulder titles were introduced in 1943; in this same year side hats began to be phased out as the standard head-dress of most English and Welsh line infantry regiments and corps.

9

**9 Sapper, Royal Engineers, 1943.** He wears a 1937 Pattern tunic and private-purchase dress side cap. He has cloth shoulder titles and the formation sign of 21st Army Group, formed in the UK on 9 July 1943 to command the 2nd British Army and 1st Canadian Army for the invasion of North Western Europe. Beneath the formation sign is the blue and red arm of service stripe worn by the Royal Engineers (not to be confused with the Royal Artillery who wore a stripe of red, then blue).

10

**10 A Classic British Tommy, annotated 1943.** In the field most soldiers removed their formation signs and insignia. He wears a shrapnel helmet, and leather jerkin with battledress blouse underneath. The helmet net dates our soldier to later in the war than 1940, few men would have looked like this during the campaigns of the western desert; I would suggest he is probably serving on campaign in Italy or Sicily. The 'look' continued later during 1944 while campaigning in North Western Europe.

11

**11 Private, 2nd Battalion, The Norfolk Regiment, India 1942.** He wears a regimental slip-on title upon his epaulette. On his sleeve is the cross keys formation badge of the 2nd Infantry Division, deployed to India in 1942. He wears a slouch hat – practical head-gear in the jungle – along with a jungle green (JG) four-pocket bush jacket. The shorts, tall socks and shoes or boots and short puttees were soon found to be the main let-down of JG and trousers were adopted and the lower half of the bush jacket tucked within.

**12 Gunner George Storey, 28th Field Regiment, Royal Artillery, India 1945.** Gunner Storey served in India and Burma and fought at Kohima. He wears a jungle green jacket and a late-war slouch hat (more the Australian style than the earlier British trilby style). This picture shows an experienced soldier who had lost almost half his body weight after suffering from dysentery, photographed shortly after discharge from 14th Army General Hospital in 1945. The author is very proud to say this is his grandfather.

12

13

**13 Guardsman, Irish Guards, 1944.** Originally black berets were only worn by members of the Tank Corps, but in 1941 the wearing of berets was extended to all units of the Royal Armoured Corps. Note the exposed buttons of his 1940 Pattern tunic.

14

**14 Trooper, Fife and Forfar Yeomanry, 1944.** His shoulder title states Royal Armoured Corps and beneath the title is the Black Bull formation sign of the 11th Armoured Division. They landed on Juno Beach on 13 June, 1944 and were deployed in all major operations of the British Second Army.

15

**15 Trooper Jack S. Woods, 9th Battalion, Royal Tank Regiment, Holland, 1944.** He wears the distinctive beret of the Royal Tank Regiment and the warm tank suit issued to armoured troops in the winter months.

16

**16 Private, Parachute Regiment, 1944.** The printed shoulder title and Pegasus date this paratrooper to the period of late 1944 to 1945. He also wears his collar open with a collar and tie, something only permitted by dress regulations for ORs while off duty from September 1944.

**17 Officer Training Unit, Royal Artillery, 1942.** During the Second World War unprecedented numbers of officers were promoted 'from the ranks'. If selected, the soldier would be sent on an Officer Training Course and while undergoing training would wear a white cap band or cover for the lower half of the side hat and white bands upon the epaulettes, as seen here.

17

**18 Second Lieutenant, King's Own Yorkshire Light Infantry, c1941.** Officers' service dress worn for light duties and parades had changed little since the end of the First World War. As battledress became widely available for all ranks, full service dress was seen far less frequently towards the later years of the Second World War.

18

**19 A wartime marriage, c1941.** The groom and his best man are brother officers in the Lincolnshire Regiment. Formation signs were occasionally worn on officers' service dress; the insignia of XI Corps Headquarters is just visible on the right arm of the best man. He also wears a cloth belt with a brass buckle instead of the leather Sam Browne.

19

**20 Warrant Officer, Highland Light Infantry, c1943.** The medal ribbons show he was entitled to the British War Medal and Victory Medal for his service in the First World War. Judging by the Territorial Force Overseas Service Medal ribbon, he had volunteered for overseas service but had been retained for home service duties (perhaps he was a member of a Territorial cyclist battalion). He was also a recipient of the Meritorious Service Medal and the Territorial Force Efficiency Medal.

21

20

**21 Captain, Royal Artillery, c1944.** As berets became popular certain units, including infantry and corps battalions, adopted the khaki beret as early as 1942.

22

**22 2nd Battalion, The Essex Regiment, Holland, 1944.** They all wear the GS beret – note the variety of styles possible. They wear a variety of 1937 and 1940 Pattern battledress and the distinctive polar bear insignia of the 49th (West Riding) Infantry Division, in which the battalion served in the 56th Infantry Brigade August 1944-1945.

23

**23 Company Sergeant Major, The King's Own Royal Regiment, Norfolk Yeomanry, 1945.** On his chest is the ribbon for the Africa Star. The open collar worn with shirt and tie and the blancoed belt with holster and pistol without cross strap, and the wearing of the beret, all point to a soldier photographed during the last year of the war. He wears the formation badge of 11th Armoured Division.

**24 Royal Engineers Officer and his Wife, 1945.** Typical of the 1945-look, our officer wears a beret and probably a tailor-made serge battledress in the 1937 Pattern (always considered far smarter than the economic 1940 Pattern; the collar is certainly faced for an officer). The date is endorsed by his medal ribbons of 1939-45 Star, France and Germany Star and Defence Medal (the latter ribbon only issued in 1945), but he wears no War Medal ribbon (a medal awarded to those who had served in the Armed Forces and Merchant Marines full-time for at least 28 days between 3 September 1939 and 2 September 1945), only issued at the very end of 1945.

24

25

**25 ATS Officer and Royal Navy Midshipman, 1941.** The ATS Second Subaltern wears a private purchase side cap with jacket and skirt of standard officers' service dress (ATS battledress was introduced in 1942). The Midshipman beside her is an officer cadet, or alternatively a commissioned officer of the lowest rank, in the Royal Navy. He is identified by the white turnback on his collar with a notched hole of white twist and button.

26

**26 Junior Rating, Royal Navy, c1940.** Unlike ordinary seamen, and sailmakers, signals, wireless telegraphy, wiremen and stokers, junior ratings wore peaked caps, jacket and trousers, with a cap badge of crown and anchor in red. The qualification badge worn on the upper right arm of this rating (crossed axe and hammer) marks him as Acting Shipwright, 4th Class, or Shipwright, 5th Class.

27

**27 Able Seaman, 1941.** A Royal Navy cap tally can reveal a fascinating history about the serviceman wearing it. HMY *Hinba* is a prime example. A danlayer, it was a type of vessel assigned to minesweeping flotillas during and immediately after the Second World War. They were usually small trawlers, fitted for the purpose of laying dans — marker buoys which consist of a long pole moored to the seabed and fitted to float vertically, usually with a coded flag at the top.

28

**28 Able Seaman George Mason, c1941.** On the back of this photograph is the annotation, 'Drowned aboard the *P.514*.' Research reveals Submarine *P.514* left the Canadian village of Argentia bound for St Johns, Newfoundland on 20 June 1942. At 0300 on the 21st the Canadian minesweeper HMCS *Georgian* was waiting to provide escort for a convoy bound for Sydney. The *Georgian*, unaware that any friendly submarines were in the area, assumed that the dark shape of *P.514* crossing her bow, was an enemy vessel and sank it. A rescue mission was immediately sent out but no survivors were found.

**29 Able Seaman, Royal Navy, c1940.** It may be deduced from this image that this man is an older sailor and as he appears to be at a training establishment, he may well have been recalled from the Reserve.

29

**30 Petty Officer, Royal Navy, c1944.** He wears the white top to his hat, at that time worn only in the summer in the UK but all year round in Mediterranean theatres. Just above his left breast pocket is the ribbon of the Africa Star with Rosette to denote the North Africa 1942-3 clasp or 'bar' awarded for service with the Royal Navy, Merchant Navy or Royal Air Force (from 23 October 1942).

30

31

**31 Lieutenant, Fleet Air Arm, 1941.** The 'A' in his cuff lace shows him to be a member of the Royal Navy Air Branch; above that are the wings of a Fleet Air Arm pilot. On his left breast he wears the ribbon of the Distinguished Service Cross, awarded to naval officers (commissioned and warrant) below the rank of Lieutenant Commander for gallantry at sea.

**32 Royal Marine in Dress Uniform, 1940.**
He is in the dark blue parade dress, worn with
dark blue and red peaked cap. He can be
identified by the globe and laurel badges worn
upon his cap and collar; the 'RM' shoulder title
can be discerned on one shoulder.

*32*

*33*

**33 Corporal, Irish Guards and
Aircraftman, RAF, c1940.** The Guards
maintained service dress on home service longer
than many other regiments and corps; the late
period of this image is suggested by the 1937
Pattern belt he is wearing, more commonly
adopted by the Guards by late 1940 (previously
they wore the 1908 web belt). The aircraftman
wears the SD tunic replaced by battledress for
air crew from 1940 and worn by all ranks and
trades from 1943.

**34 Royal Air Force Officer, 1940.** This is the classic image of an early war fighter pilot. He wears four-pocket service dress with collar and tie, above his left pocket are his RAF pilot wings and on his collar are the brass letters 'VR' which denote him a member of the RAF Volunteer Reserve. The lack of shiny peak and gold oak leaves on his cap, denoting an officer of Air rank, means this man could only be an officer ranked between Pilot Officer and Squadron Leader. Some fighter pilots left their top button undone (especially when walking out) to differentiate themselves from bomber pilots.

34

*35*

**35 Sergeant Pilot, RAF, c1940.** From 1940 aircrew could qualify as pilots; they continued to wear the hairy serge tunic but would be entitled to wear the wings and fulfil the duties of fighter or bomber pilot. The 'VR' beneath his shoulder eagle denotes him as a member of the Volunteer Reserve.

**36 Aircrew in Training as a Pilot, 1940-41.** When a man volunteered and was selected to go through his training as a pilot, his status was denoted by a white peak inserted into his side hat. Some of them were sent abroad to train in places with safe airspace such as Canada, Oklahoma USA, and Rhodesia. Many brave potential pilots were killed in accidents and through error while learning to fly during the Second World War.

*36*

37

**37 Aircraftman, RAF, 1940.** Note the brass cap badge and shoulder eagles worn by RAF groundcrew.; also, the vogue of 1940 to be photographed in greatcoat with collar open and turned up.

**38 RAF Sergeant Observer, c1941.** He wears the battledress jacket and trousers for aircrew from 1940 and worn by all ranks and trades from 1943, and the 'O' brevet of a qualified Observer. Originally adopted in 1915 by the RFC, this badge continued to be used by the RAF until superseded by the Navigators' and Air Bombers' badges in 1942.

*38*

*39*

**39 Sergeant, Royal Air Force c1942.** He wears the brevet of the Air Gunner, adopted in 1939 when the role of Air Gunner became a full-time category of aircrew. Air Gunners who also acted as wireless operators wore the Wireless Operators sleeve badge; this configuration was later replaced by a 'WAG' brevet. Aircrew were also issued with whistles of the Acme Thunderer type and wore them with some pride from the loops at the collar of their battledress; this was particularly observed by the crews of Coastal Command and Bomber Command.

40

**40 Sister, Queen Alexandra's Imperial Military Nursing Service Reserve, 1940.** Her status as a member of the reserve is denoted by the QAIMNS 'R' Reserve medallion she wears.

**41 ATS Sergeant and Officer, c1941.** The ATS sergeant's uniform would have been made of a wool serge of a slightly better quality and greener colour than soldiers' battledress; her cap badge and shoulder insignia would be in brass. Although absent in this photograph, a fabric belt with a brass buckle would normally be worn with the jacket. The officer would have her uniform made from smart officer's serge, would not wear 'ATS' on her shoulder but would have a bronzed cap and collar badges; all ranks wear a collar and tie.

41

*42*

**42 Corporal, ATS, c1941.** Although issued with a peaked cap similar to those of the drivers in the women's forces during the First World War, our smartly turned out corporal is wearing a private-purchase side cap, which would have had a beech-brown crown piped with green.

*43*

**43 Private, ATS, 1941.** She is wearing the early-war peaked cap with fabric chin strap (leather chin straps were introduced in 1941). Note the Royal Artillery white lanyard (on her right) and grenade on her left breast. This denoted the unit she was serving with. Royal Artillery and Royal Corps of Signals are frequently seen but many ATS attached to line infantry were also granted the honour of wearing their badges on the left breast – the ATS cap badge always remained. On the upper sleeves of many ATS tunics, formation signs are often displayed.

44

**44 A Women's Royal Naval Service 'Wren' Rating, c1941.** She wears a cap with white cover, worn during the summer months. The duties of Wrens in the Second World War embraced all those of the original WRNS and expanded them to a vast array of skilled jobs from target operators, torpedoes and air mechanic electricians to radio operators, coders and transcribers.

45

**45 Aircraftwoman Second Class, Women's Auxiliary Air Force c1941.** The WAAF was created in June 1939, taking in the RAF companies of the Auxiliary Territorial Service.

*46*

**46 Home Guard Major, Norfolk, 1941.** On his shoulder can be seen the crown which designates him a Major. Below that is the shoulder title 'Home Guard'; his county designation letters are obscured but his cap badge shows he is Norfolk Regiment and we can discern he is part of the 5th Battalion, Norfolk Home Guard. Research reveals they were based in North Walsham with platoons from around the immediate district.

*47*

**47 Sergeant Patient, Essex Home Guard, c1944.** He is wearing above and below county Home Guard designation and battalion number – ESX 19, denoting he is part of 19th (Grays) Battalion, Essex Home Guard.

*48*

**48 Lance Corporal, Lincolnshire Home Guard, c1942.** His cap badge shows he is Lincolnshire Home Guard and he wears the standard HG equipment of BAR (Browning Automatic Rifle) pouches with leather belt and webbing cross straps. His gas mask is being worn in the slung position from right shoulder to left side (although he would be advised to wear the haversack over his webbing if the gas mask needs to be worn in the alert position on his chest). His single stripes denote him a Lance Corporal; he is holding a P.14 or P.17 rifle used by HG units, and wearing a pair of leather gaiters.

# Appendix I

## The 99 British Line Infantry Regiments in 1865

1st   Regiment of Foot (The Royal Scots)
2nd   (The Queen's Royal) Regiment of Foot
3rd   Regiment of Foot (East Kent Regiment of Foot) (The Buffs)
4th   (The King's Own) Regiment of Foot
5th   Regiment of Foot (The Northumberland Regiment of Foot)
6th   Regiment of Foot (1st Royal Warwickshire Regiment of Foot)
7th   Royal Fusiliers (Royal Fusiliers)
8th   (The King's) Regiment of Foot (The King's Regiment of Foot)
9th   Regiment of Foot (The East Norfolk Regiment of Foot)
10th  Regiment of Foot (The North Lincolnshire Regiment of Foot)
11th  Regiment of Foot (The North Devonshire Regiment of Foot)
12th  Regiment of Foot (The East Suffolk Regiment of Foot)
13th  Regiment of Foot (1st Somersetshire Light Infantry Regiment of Foot)
14th  Regiment of Foot (Bedfordshire Regiment of Foot/Buckinghamshire Regiment of Foot)
15th  Regiment of Foot (The Yorkshire East Riding Regiment of Foot)
16th  Regiment of Foot (Bedfordshire Regiment of Foot/The Buckinghamshire Regiment of Foot)
17th  Regiment of Foot (The Leicestershire Regiment of Foot)
18th  Regiment of Foot (The Royal Irish Regiment of Foot)
19th  Regiment of Foot (1st North Yorkshire Riding Regiment of Foot)
20th  Regiment of Foot (East Devonshire Regiment of Foot)
21st  Regiment of Foot (Royal Scots Fusiliers Regiment of Foot)
22nd  Regiment of Foot (The Cheshire Regiment of Foot)
23rd  Regiment of Foot (Royal Welch Fusiliers)
24th  Regiment of Foot (2nd Warwickshire Regiment of Foot)
25th  Regiment of Foot (King's Own Borderers Regiment of Foot)
26th  Regiment of Foot (The Cameronian Regiment of Foot)
27th  Regiment of Foot (Inniskilling Regiment of Foot)
28th  Regiment of Foot (North Gloucestershire Regiment of Foot)
29th  Regiment of Foot (Worcestershire Regiment of Foot)
30th  Regiment of Foot (Cambridgeshire Regiment of Foot)
31st  Regiment of Foot (Huntingdonshire Regiment of Foot)
32nd  Regiment of Foot (Cornwall Regiment of Foot)
33rd  Regiment of Foot (1st Yorkshire West Riding Regiment of Foot)
34th  Regiment of Foot (Cumberland Regiment of Foot)
35th  Regiment of Foot (Dorsetshire Regiment of Foot/Sussex Regiment of Foot)
36th  Regiment of Foot (Herefordshire Regiment of Foot)
37th  Regiment of Foot (North Hampshire Regiment of Foot)
38th  Regiment of Foot (1st Staffordshire Regiment of Foot)
39th  Regiment of Foot (Dorsetshire Regiment of Foot/East Middlesex Regiment of Foot)
40th  Regiment of Foot (2nd Somersetshire Regiment of Foot)
41st  Regiment of Foot (Welsh Regiment of Foot)

42nd Regiment of Foot (Royal Highland Regiment of Foot)

43rd Regiment of Foot (Royal Highland Regiment of Foot/Monmouthshire Regiment of Foot)

44th Regiment of Foot (East Essex Regiment of Foot)

45th Regiment of Foot (Nottinghamshire Regiment of Foot)

46th Regiment of Foot (South Devonshire Regiment of Foot)

47th Regiment of Foot (Lancashire Regiment of Foot)

48th Regiment of Foot (Northamptonshire Regiment of Foot)

49th Regiment of Foot (Hertfordshire Regiment of Foot)

50th Regiment of Foot (The Queen's Own Regiment of Foot)

51st Regiment of Foot (2nd Yorkshire West Riding Regiment of Foot)

52nd Regiment of Foot (Oxfordshire Regiment of Foot (Light Infantry)

53rd Regiment of Foot (Shropshire Regiment of Foot)

54th Regiment of Foot (West Norfolk Regiment of Foot)

55th Regiment of Foot (Westmoreland Regiment of Foot)

56th Regiment of Foot (West Essex Regiment of Foot)

57th Regiment of Foot (West Middlesex Regiment of Foot)

58th Regiment of Foot (Rutlandshire Regiment of Foot)

59th Regiment of Foot (2nd Nottingham Regiment of Foot)

60th Regiment of Foot (The King's Royal Rifle Corps Regiment of Foot)

61st Regiment of Foot (South Gloucestershire Regiment of Foot)

62nd Regiment of Foot (Royal American Regiment of Foot/Wiltshire Regiment of Foot)

63rd Regiment of Foot (West Suffolk Regiment of Foot)

64th Regiment of Foot (2nd Staffordshire Regiment of Foot)

65th Regiment of Foot (2nd Yorkshire North Riding Regiment of Foot)

66th Regiment of Foot (Berkshire Regiment of Foot)

67th Regiment of Foot (South Hampshire Regiment of Foot)

68th Regiment of Foot (Durham Regiment of Foot (Light Infantry))

69th Regiment of Foot (South Lincolnshire Regiment of Foot)

70th Regiment of Foot (Surrey Regiment of Foot)

71st Regiment of Foot (Glasgow Highland Regiment of Foot)

72nd Regiment of Foot (Duke of Albany's Own Regiment of Foot)

73rd Regiment of Foot (Perthshire Regiment of Foot)

74th Regiment of Foot (Highland Regiment of Foot)

75th Regiment of Foot (Gordon Highlanders )

76th Regiment of Foot (East India Company)

77th Regiment of Foot (East Middlesex Regiment of Foot)

78th Regiment of Foot (Seaforth Highlander Regiment)

79th Regiment of Foot (Cameronian Regiment of Foot)

80th Regiment of Foot (Royal Edinburgh Volunteers/Staffordshire Volunteers)

81st Regiment of Foot (Loyal Lincoln Volunteers Regiment of Foot)

82nd Regiment of Foot (Prince of Wales' Volunteers)

83rd Regiment of Foot (County of Dublin Regiment of Foot)

84th Regiment of Foot (York and Lancaster Regiment of Foot)

85th  Regiment of Foot (The King's Regiment of Light Infantry (Bucks Volunteers))
86th  Regiment of Foot (Royal County Down Regiment of Foot)
87th  Regiment of Foot (The Prince of Wales' Irish Regiment of Foot)
88th  Regiment of Foot (Connaught Rangers)
89th  Regiment of Foot (The Princess Victoria's Regiment of Foot)
90th  Regiment of Foot (Perthshire Volunteers (Light Infantry)
91st  Regiment of Foot (Argyllshire Regiment of Foot)
92nd Regiment of Foot (Gordon Highlanders Regiment of Foot)
93rd  Regiment of Foot (Sutherland Highlanders Regiment of Foot)
94th  Regiment of Foot (Royal Welsh Volunteers)
95th  Regiment of Foot (The Prince Consort's Own Rifle Brigade)
96th  Regiment of Foot (Queen's Own Germans)
97th  Regiment of Foot (Earl of Ulster's Regiment of Foot)
98th  Regiment of Foot (Prince of Wales' Regiment of Foot)
99th  Regiment of Foot (Lanarkshire Regiment of Foot)

# *Appendix II*

## County Designations of the Home Guard in the Second World War

| | | | |
|---|---|---|---|
| A | Anglesey | FT | Flintshire |
| AB | Aberdeenshire and City Of Aberdeen | G | City of Glasgow |
| ABK | Aberdeenshire (Kincardineshire BN) | GLN | Glamorganshire |
| ANG | Angus | GLS | Gloucestershire |
| ARG | Argyllshire | H | Hampshire & Isle of Wight |
| AYR | Ayrshire | HD | Lincolnshire (Holland) |
| BDF | Bedfordshire | HDS | Huntingdonshire |
| BHM | Warwickshire (Birmingham) | HFD | Herefordshire |
| BNF | Banffshire | HTS | Hertfordshire |
| BR | Brecknockshire | IOM | Isle of Man |
| BRX | Berkshire | IN | Inverness-shire (Nairnshire Bn) |
| BUX | Buckinghamshire | INV | Inverness-shire |
| CA | Caithness | K | Lincolnshire (Kesteven) |
| CAM | Cambridgeshire | KT | Kent |
| CC | Caernarvonshire | L | Lincolnshire (Lindsey) |
| CDN | Cardiganshire | LEI | Leicestershire |
| CH | Cheshire | LF | Lancashire (21 22 27, 41-3, 55, 60, 64 Btns) |
| CLN | Clackmannanshire | | |
| CO | Cornwall | LK | Lanarkshire |
| COL | City of London | LON | County of London |
| COV | Warwickshire (Coventry) | LR | Lancashire |
| CRM | Carmarthenshire | M | Merioneth & Montgomery |
| CT | Lincolnshire (Lincoln – county town) | MAN | Lancashire (23, 25, 26, 44-51, 56, 61, 63 Btns) |
| CUM | Cumberland | | |
| DBT | Dumbartonshire | ML | Midlothian |
| DDE | City of Dundee | MON | Monmouthshire |
| DEN | Denbighshire | MRY | Moray |
| DFS | Dumfriesshire | MX | Middlesex |
| DHM | Durham | ND | Northumberland |
| DOR | Dorset | NK | Norfolk |
| DVN | Devon | NN | Northamptonshire |
| EHG | City of Edinburgh | NRY | North Riding of Yorkshire |
| EL | Lancashire I(1-15, 28-32, 57-59, and 62 Bns) | NS | North Staffordshire |
| | | NTS | Nottinghamshire |
| EL | East Lothian | ORK | Orkney |
| ELY | Isle of Ely | OXF | Oxfordshire |
| ER | East Riding of Yorkshire | PEM | Pembrokeshire |
| ESX | Essex | R | Ross-shire |
| F | Fife | R&B | Renfrewshire & Buteshire Bn |

REN   Renfrewshire
R-L   Ross-shire (Lewis Bn)
RR   Radnorshire
RU   Rutland
SB   Scottish Border
SF   Derbyshire
SFK   Suffolk
SHR   Shropshire
SKR   Stewartry of Kirkcudbrightshire
SOM   Somerset
SS   South Staffordshire
STG   Stirlingshire
SU   Sutherland
SX   Sussex
SY   Surrey
TAY   Perthshire
TWD   Peebleshire
UTP   Upper Thames Patrol
WAR   Warwickshire
WES   Westmorland
WL   West Lancashire
WL   West Lothian
WNM   Wigtownshire (Machars Btn)
WNR   Wigtownshire (Rhinns Bat)
WOR   Worcestershire
WR   West Riding of Yorkshire
WTS   Wiltshire
Z   Zetland

# Select Bibliography

Chappell, Mike, *British Battle Insignia 1 1919-18* (Osprey, 1986)

Chappell, Mike, *British Battle Insignia 2 1939-45* (Osprey, 1994)

Chappell, Mike, *British Infantry Equipments 1808-1908* (Osprey, 1980)

Chappell, Mike, *British Infantry Equipments 1908-80* (Osprey, 1989)

Collett Wadge, D, (ed.) *Women in Uniform* (Imperial War Museum, 2003)

Cormack, Andrew and Cormack, Peter, *British Air Forces 1914-18 (1)* (Osprey, 2000)

Cox, Reginald H. W., *Military Badges of the British Empire* (Ernest Benn, 1982)

Ferguson, Gregor, *The Paras: British Airborne Forces 1940-1984* (Osprey, 1984)

Flower, Newman, (ed.) *The History of The Great War* (London, 1919)

Forty, George, *The British Army Handbook 1939-1945* (Chancellor, 2000)

Fosten, D.S.V., *The British Army 1914-18* (Osprey, 1986)

Gaylor, John, *Military Badge Collecting* (Leo Cooper, 1991)

James, Brigadier E.A., *British Regiments 1914-18* (Naval & Military Press, 1993)

Jewell, Brian, *British Battledress 1937-61* (Osprey, 1981)

Longmate, Norman, *The Real Dad's Army* (Hutchinson, 1974)

Mills, Jon, *From Scarlet to Khaki* (Wardens Publishing, 2005)

Rawson, Andrew, *British Army Handbook 1914-1918* (Sutton, 2006)

Richards, Walter, *His Majesty's Territorial Army* (London, c1910)

Rosignoli, Guido, *Badges and Insignia of World War II (Air Force, Naval and Marine)* (Blandford, 1980)

Sellwood, A.V., The *Saturday Night Soldiers: The stirring story of the Territorial Army* (London, 1966)

Swinnerton, Iain, *Identifying your World War I Soldier from Badges and Photographs* (Federation of Family History Societies Publications Ltd, 2001)

Wallace, Edgar, *Kitchener's Army and the Territorial Forces* (London, 1914-15)

Westlake, Ray, *British Territorial Units 1914-18* (Osprey, 1991)

Westlake, Ray, *Collecting Metal Shoulder Titles* (Leo Cooper, 1997)

Westlake, Ray, *Kitchener's Army* (Spellmount, 2003)

Westlake, Ray, *The Territorial Battalions* (Tunbridge Wells, 1986)

Whittaker, L.B., *Stand Down* (Westlake, 1990)

Articles by the author and Iain Swinnerton published in *Family Tree Magazine* on Dress Regulations for the Royal Navy, the British Army, the Territorial Force and the Royal Air Force (various dates)

# Internet Resources

The Long, Long Trail – The British Army 1914-1918 for family historians:
www.1914-1918.net/index.html

Find and start to research the fallen of both wars with the Commonwealth War Graves Commission Debt of Honour Register:
www.cwgc.org/debt_of_honour.asp

A very useful Victoria Cross website:
www.victoriacross.org.uk/vcross.htm

Database of all recipients of the George Cross:
www.gc-database.co.uk/alpha.htm

Hints on researching British Prisoners of War in the First World War:
www.btinternet.com/~prosearch/tomspage19.html

Badges and insignia of the Royal Navy in the Second World War:
www.naval-history.net/WW2aaRN-PayTables00Ranks-Badges.htm

A reliable and well researched site for researching naval actions, Royal Navy (incl. submarines) and Merchant Navy losses:
www.uboat.net/index.html

A useful article on Royal Navy cap tallies:
www.nhcra-online.org/19c/captallies.htm

Useful site to help identify British Formation badges of the Second World War:
www.petergh.f2s.com/flashes.html

Short history and ranks of the ATS:
en.wikipedia.org/wiki/Auxiliary_Territorial_Service

Useful site for those researching military nurses:
www.scarletfinders.co.uk/8.html

# Index